D1006247

KIDS OF KABUL

KIDS OF KABUL
LIVING BRAVELY THROUGH A NEVER-ENDING WAR
DEBORAH ELLIS

GROUNDWOOD BOOKS / HOUSE OF ANANSI PRESS
TORONTO BERKELEY

Groundwood Books / House of Anansi Press
110 Spadina Avenue, Suite 801, Toronto, Ontario M5V 2K4
or c/o Publishers Group West
1700 Fourth Street, Berkeley, CA 94710

We acknowledge for their financial support of our publishing program
the Canada Council for the Arts, the Government of Canada through the
Canada Book Fund (CBF) and the Ontario Arts Council.

 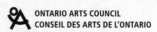

Canada Council   Conseil des Arts
for the Arts   du Canada

ONTARIO ARTS COUNCIL
CONSEIL DES ARTS DE L'ONTARIO

Library and Archives Canada Cataloguing in Publication

Ellis, Deborah
Kids of Kabul : living bravely through a never-ending war / Deborah Ellis.

ISBN 978-1-55498-181-6

1. Children–Afghanistan–Juvenile literature. 2. Children and war–
Afghanistan–Juvenile literature. 3. Afghan War, 2001- –Children–Juvenile
literature. I. Title.
HQ792.A3E55 2012   j305.235092'2581   C2011-906638-6

Front cover photo: Gilles Bassignac / Gamma-Rapho via Getty Images
Back cover photo: Paula Bronstein / Getty Images
All other photos are courtesy of the author.
Design by Michael Solomon

Groundwood Books is committed to protecting our natural environment.
As part of our efforts, the interior of this book is printed on paper that
contains 100% post-consumer recycled fibers, is acid-free and is
processed chlorine-free.

Printed and bound in Canada

To the next generation of survivors

Introduction

I am a feminist, which means I believe that women are of equal value to men. I am from Canada, a country not without its struggles but where women and girls are not limited — in theory — by the fact that they are female. When I heard about the Taliban takeover of Afghanistan in 1996, and the crimes they perpetrated against women and girls, I decided to get involved.

This started me on a journey that has taken me from Afghan refugee communities in Canada to the muddy tent camps in Pakistan and the decrepit Soviet workers' holiday hotels outside Moscow that, ten years ago, served as encampments for Afghan and other refugees. It is a journey that has spawned four books: an adult book (*Women of the Afghan War*) and three novels about children under the Taliban, the last one published in 2003.

And now I've gone back.

Afghanistan has been at war for decades. It has been used by the world's great powers in their struggles against each other. One such struggle produced the Taliban government, which, at an earlier stage of the war, had been supported by the United States. Among other things, the Taliban regime was brutally repressive toward women. The Taliban also harbored al-Qaeda, the terrorists who were responsible for the September 11th attacks on the United States in 2001. The war that followed initially overthrew the Taliban government but has continued for the past eleven years.

The real losers are the Afghan people, especially the women and children. Their daily lives are still threatened by suicide bombings, armed conflict and other forms of violence, and even Kabul, the capital city, is not secure. Tens of thousands of Afghans have died since 9/11 — many, many more than died in the twin towers. People have been injured, maimed, displaced and terrorized. People are hungry, people are fleeing, and families are separated from their homes and from each other. Refugees who left their homes as long as twenty years ago live in informal camps where they have no services other than those offered by one or two NGOs. This means there are still millions of internally and externally displaced Afghans living in miserable conditions without water, plumbing or electricity. The billions and billions of dollars spent on the war, which might have been spent on education, health care, housing and rebuilding a civil society, have been spent on weapons.

So has anything been gained?

For some young people life has improved, and they are grabbing hold of every opportunity with both hands. Though more than half the children in Afghanistan still have no access to schooling, those who do study hard. When they are allowed to play sports, they play hard. The lucky ones who have money and who live in Kabul and a few other cities are reaching out to each other and to the

Children's playground in a park just north of Kabul.

world, using social media and new technologies. Some institutions are bringing them into contact with music and art. And they are finding ways to take their considerable energies and talents into public life to move their country forward.

The interviews in this book were conducted over the weeks I was in Kabul early in 2011. Many of the young people spoke only Afghan languages, so their words were translated into English for me by an interpreter — the same interpreter for many of the interviews.

Although I usually travel alone, this time I traveled with Janice Eisenhauer and Lauryn Oates from Canadian Women for Women in Afghanistan. Many of the places I visited were involved with projects funded by Women for Women. Due to the security situation, I did not travel beyond Kabul.

It is possible to read the interviews in this book and come away feeling hopeful about the future of these kids and the future of their country. It is good to be hopeful, and if the future could be in the hands of this generation of young people, with their eagerness, openness and determination, then Afghanistan could indeed be a garden again.

Sadly, the old way of doing things — the way of corruption and killing and suspicion and venal international interests — seems to be gaining the upper hand. But there is no question that we must reach out and support these young people and the Afghan organizations that work with them. Only through work at the grassroots level can the patient day-to-day of rebuilding take place.

We have to stand together to move forward. Anything we can do to connect with Afghan people, to appreciate what they have been through and what they are capable of, and to assist them in getting the education they need to rebuild their own country will be a step away from madness and pain, and a step toward the sunshine.

Deborah Ellis
2012

AFGHANISTAN

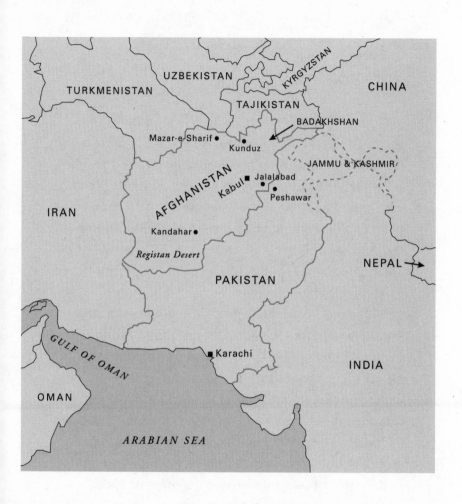

Faranoz, 14

During the Taliban regime, schools for girls were closed, and women were forbidden from attending university. Extreme poverty coupled with decades of war and chaos have left the country with high rates of illiteracy. According to the United Nations Human Development Report of 2008, only 28 percent of Afghan adults can read and write. That number drops to 13 percent for women.

Since the fall of the Taliban, the international community has partnered with the people of Afghanistan to raise literacy levels and encourage education for all. It is an uphill struggle — one undertaken at times with enthusiasm and at times with suspicion. In addition to regular schools, literacy classes have been introduced into non-traditional spaces to make them as accessible and acceptable as possible.

A small house in a rundown area of Kabul is a gathering point for widows and their daughters. The women have all experienced trauma brought on by the war and related violence. After receiving counseling for a few months, they take part in literacy classes. Each step forward gives them more power over their own lives.

The women crowd into a low-ceilinged room with walls decorated with the handicrafts they have made. They sit on toshaks along the walls, and when those are filled, they move into any available space on the floor. A small woodstove takes the chill out of the winter air.

Faranoz comes here with her mother. She has seven sisters and three brothers.

Everyone says I have too much intelligence. They laugh when they say it, so it is a joke, but they are right. I am very smart.

A year ago, I could not read anything at all, but now I can read all sorts of things — books, poems, everything. I can write, too. This proves I am smart.

I live in a poor area of Kabul. My father died thirteen years ago. No one in this room has a father or husband. The men died in the war or from sickness or they were murdered. Husbands and fathers die for all sorts of reasons. Some get shot. Sometimes there are road accidents. Some fathers go to Iran or to Pakistan to look for work and don't come back.

My mother has no job, so we are very poor. My oldest brother is in charge of us. He is the one who said I should not go to school, so that is why I spent so many years not knowing how to read. I don't know why he said no school for me. Does he have to give a reason? Maybe he doesn't think I am smart enough for school. Maybe he is afraid I would end up smarter than him, and then how would he be able to tell me what to do? The women in this class have all been through bad times in the war. I was very small when the war ended but I hear everyone talk about it.

Our lessons are supposed to last one and a half hours, but they often go longer because the women want to talk about their problems. But that was more in the beginning. As they become better at reading they want to talk more about reading and less about the things that make them sad.

This meeting room is really just a room in a woman's house. The woman used to be married to a man who belonged to the Taliban. He was a very bad man. He beat her and made her be with other men, a very disrespectful thing. But she was very brave. She went to the Supreme Court and got a divorce. I don't know when this was. Sometime after the war. This is her brother's house. She lives here and he lets her have this room for us to meet.

Our teacher is a lawyer as well as a teacher. She has told us about how she defended women who were being beaten or treated badly. She says important people have offered her important jobs, but she prefers to be here in this room with us, because we are important, too.

The first day of classes, many women were crying because their lives are so hard and no one ever asks them about that. They don't get to just come and sit and talk with other women. They are expected to just live their lives and be quiet. But the teacher here started to ask them and that's when they started to cry. Some would not talk at all at first. Even I was too afraid to shake the teacher's hand or even to look at her. I was afraid that she would see that I was not smart. But now I know I am smart, so I am not afraid anymore.

After a year of learning to read, we are all different people. We can stand up straight and read out the words we have written in loud clear voices. We laugh more than we cry.

Even though I am young, I know many things. Sometimes the older women forget I'm in the room, and they talk as if I'm not here. I hear all about their lives, about their children who died or their husbands who hit them.

I know that some women did not tell their families they were coming here. They said they were going to the market or to a clinic, or they only came to class when no one was at home to stop them. Only after many months

The courtyard of a home where literacy classes are held.

had passed did they tell them, and by then they could read some things, so their families said, "You are using your time well, you are learning something, you are happier, okay, you can continue to go."

The books we most like to read are about law, the constitution and about religion. Through these books we learn that we have rights. And if our families disagree, we can point to the book and say, "Here! It is written down! The law must be respected!" Religion does not give men the right to beat us, and now we can prove it.

Some of the stories are funny now, because we know better, but they weren't funny when they happened. One woman says she got a prescription from the doctor and she got it mixed up with other papers, and what she took to the pharmacy was not the prescription, it was the electric bill! Women talk about how they used to be like blind, but reading has made them able to see.

I used to think, if only I could read, then I would be happy. But now I just want more! I want to read about poets and Afghan history and science and about places outside Afghanistan. Many of us write our own stories, and we decorate the borders of the pages with drawings of flowers and designs, because that is the Afghan tradition.

My brother lets me come here because it's not really a school. More just a place where women get together to learn. My mother was the first to come, and when he saw that she felt better and seemed happier, he said, okay, it would not be bad if I came with her. There are only women here, so he thinks I won't get into trouble and make him look bad.

I hope he lets me go to a proper school one day because I like to be around books and I would like to be a doctor one day. I think I would be a good doctor. What else can I do with so much intelligence!

Liza, 16

A tradition of Islamic art — or art created in the Islamic world, regardless of the religion of the creator — involves creating a sense of balance and harmony. One part of the tradition is to focus on patterns rather than representations of living creatures. The magnificent tile work on mosques and public spaces throughout the Middle East is a testament to the grandeur of this style of work.

Other traditions, such as the one led by the great Afghan miniaturist of the sixteenth century, Kamal al-Din Bihzad, created spectacular illuminated books of illustrated poetry and legends, with people and even the Prophet Muhammad represented in full-face drawings.

The first national Afghan school of fine arts was established in 1921, with other schools coming along as the decades passed and leaders changed. When the Taliban took power, art was one of the many forms of self-expression they crushed. They even destroyed many of Afghanistan's artistic and cultural treasures, such as the giant Buddhas of Bamiyan (magnificent giant statues carved into the side of a cliff and deliberately dynamited by the Taliban in 2001). Most forms of art were against the law.

In one of the many attempts to rescue and rebuild the cultural life of Afghanistan, a women's art center was established by the Centre for Contemporary Arts Afghanistan (CCAA). Since 2006 it has trained hundreds of young Afghan women in painting, photography and filmmaking. After living in a time when their voices were silenced, having ability in the arts allows women and girls like Liza to express themselves in new and daring ways.

I live with my mother and one sister. My father died from an untreated illness some time ago. When he got ill, there was no doctor and no medicine. We could see he was sick and suffering, and we did what we could to try to keep him warm and comfortable, but the pain was bad and we watched him die. We were all helpless.

To lose a father in Afghanistan is a dangerous thing because it is very hard for a woman to earn enough money on her own to support herself and her children. She has to rely on someone to help her — an uncle, a brother — and that makes her like a beggar.

For my family it has been very hard. I was seven when my father died. He used to work in a shop selling carpets. I remember visiting him there to take him some lunch. It was the time of the Taliban, so my mother could not go outside with any safety. The Taliban would beat her if they saw her. It was a little safer for me because I was a little child, and they usually ignored very little children. The shop was near to where we lived and I would run there and back. I ran because I was afraid of them. But I was glad to get out.

Except for taking the lunch, we just sat inside. No school, no playing. Nothing. The days were long and we would argue just for something to do. When you are locked up with someone, everything they do can quickly become annoying, because you can't get away from it. Every day is the same.

Before the Taliban fell there was a lot of fighting and shooting. It was terrible. But then it stopped and things are better now. I am about to start grade ten. I study very hard in school. We are on school break now for the winter. Instead of going to regular school classes I come here every day to work on learning art.

After the Taliban, my family was really hopeful. People would come to visit and I'd hear them talk. "The dark period is over," they'd say. "We can all breathe again." But it's

A sculpture in the courtyard of the women's art center.

not really like that. We can do some things, but we never know who is watching and who will try to stop us with violence or by saying bad things. I try not to think about it. I prefer to think about art.

I am just beginning to learn about it. I've been learning about colors and shapes and how to use light and shadow. When I look around at some of the work done by women who have studied for a while, I think, "How can they do that?" Then I think that one day a new student will ask the same thing about my work, because I will be so good at it.

Many girls paint their memories or their thoughts about their memories. How do they feel when they remember this thing? That's what they paint. So when you see their painting, you get their feeling.

The older artists paint sadder, darker pictures than the younger artists like me. Of course, we are still learning technique and have a long way to go in our studies, but I think we are looking more to the future than to the past. I have heard many sad stories, and I know there are many more, too many more. I want to think about happier things and put my mind and my art to making work that will give people a good feeling instead of a dark feeling. We all have things inside us that need to come out. It can be dangerous to speak, or maybe you are too shy to speak. But you can draw your feelings, in private, and let them out.

We have all lost things because of the war. Losing things and people is normal for Afghans. We have had enough of that. It is time to plan for good days and before you can do that, you have to fill your head with thoughts that are hopeful.

That is why I like to paint the ocean. I have never seen the ocean for real. One day I will, when I travel the world as a famous artist. I paint it because when you look at the ocean, nothing gets in your way. There are no obstacles. You can see forever.

This is what we want for Afghanistan — no more obstacles!

Aman, 16

Poverty and child labor go together. War creates poverty. War creates situations where families are so desperate for food and shelter that children must work to provide these necessities, especially if their parents have been killed or maimed by the conflict. War also destroys schools, and when schools are destroyed, opportunities for a way out of bone-grinding poverty are destroyed.

In Afghanistan, children are engaged in all sorts of work, from water-carrying to sheep-herding to carpet-weaving and working in shops. The money they earn goes to basic necessities like bread, and a hard day's work nets them barely enough to keep starvation at bay. And if they don't work, they don't eat.

Aman is one of the lucky ones. He landed at a school that educates child workers and others from very poor families. The school is down a chopped-up, muddy alley in a slum district of the city. It is surrounded by high walls. It looks shabby compared to schools in North America, but inside it is a safe haven, a powerhouse of young minds reaching for something better.

I lost fifteen members of my family to the Taliban, including my parents. We were living in Kabul. Not in a rich neighborhood. Lots of poor families. The Taliban came and said to my father, "What is your name?" He told them and then they killed him. Then they killed my mother. Then they kept on killing until fifteen members of my family were dead. I am alive and my little sister and my grandfather are alive. My grandfather is disabled and lives a very poor life. So I live here at this school with my sister.

I am now in grade nine and I am at the top of my class. I want to be a doctor, of course. This is the dream of many Afghans because we have seen so much death and suffering.

I did not begin school at the correct time in my life because I had to work. When I was young I was a shepherd and looked after sheep that belonged to someone else. My

A computer room at a school for impoverished and working children.

job was to keep the sheep together in the street and take them from one garbage dump to another so they could rub their noses through the plastic bags and things people threw away. That was how they would eat. They had to eat garbage because we have no grass in Kabul except in the parks and they were far away from where I lived and they don't allow sheep. Everything else is dust and rock.

It isn't a hard job, looking after sheep, but I was very small at the time. It seemed hard to me then. The sheep were bigger than me! I was always afraid they would not go where I told them to go. If I lost one, it would have gone very bad. It doesn't matter whether I liked it or not. It was my job and I had to do it.

If I wasn't able to go to school that might still be my

life, taking sheep from one garbage place to another. So I study hard and I work hard. I have no free time. Every hour is busy.

I help teach the younger boys here. Most of them also have jobs. This one is a mechanic, this one goes through garbage, this one helps out in a shop. They work in the morning. Then they come here for a free lunch and stay for classes. Many of the boys here earn money to support their whole families, so they have to work. If they don't work, no one eats. The free meal they get here at the school for lunch makes their family feel better about them spending the afternoon at classes instead of at more work.

When I miss my family, so much that my chest hurts and everything hurts, I try to calm myself by thinking of my future, because I think it could be a good future if no one comes in and starts killing again. Look at what I've learned in just a few years! When I first came here I was afraid all the time. I had too many dark, sad things in my head. I thought there would never be room there for anything else. Then I learned how to read and write and even to use a computer. So now I have many good things to think about.

I don't know why the Taliban killed my family. My family were innocent. They were not important, fancy people. They were nobody's enemies. The Taliban killed my family just to show their power. They did a lot of that, killing whole families. You can see it when you go into a graveyard. Big groups of family members all buried on the same day. Like they are on a picnic. Only they are dead.

Karima, 14

Women need economic power. Economic power means having ownership over enough money to create their own lives, to live without being dependent on men for food, shelter and the other necessities of life. This is true for women everywhere.

In North America there are laws to protect the rights of women and, just as important, there are strong social customs to back those laws up. When Canadian and American women are beaten by their male partners, there are shelters for them to go to with their children, and the police can arrest the men for assault. The system doesn't always work the way it is supposed to, and each year women are still murdered by their male partners. But the ideal we strive for is that no one has the right to make anyone else live in a state of fear. And since women in North America have the right to earn their own money — and decide how to spend it — they can learn to make the types of choices that will help them avoid or get away from abusive men.

In Afghanistan social customs make it very difficult for women to have independent economic power, and without that, they must depend on men for their survival. Very often this turns out fine, as the vast majority of Afghan men — like men anywhere — are kind and strive to do the right thing. But when a woman is forced to be dependent on an abusive man, her choices are often limited. She can suffer through it and hope things get better, she can commit suicide, she can escape the home and hope she is not found and killed for "dishonoring" her family, or she can kill the abuser and be executed or spend the rest of her life in prison.

Karima and her mother face this situation every day of their lives.

My father has been dead for ten years. He died of a brain attack. My mother washes clothes for people in the neighborhood, and they give her a little money. It is not enough to live on. We live in a poor area and the neighbors can't pay a lot.

I have three sisters and one brother. My brother is seven and the youngest. We live with my mother's brother, my uncle. He has just a small house — one room we share with his family. There are too many of us in that small space, but where else can we go?

There are not enough mats for us all to sleep on, so my family sleeps on the floor. There is a rug but it is thin, and the floor is a cold and hard place to sleep. The house has no electricity. None of the houses in the area do. When it becomes dark outside it becomes dark inside. I have no way to do my homework.

My uncle has oil lamps and candles, but when I try to use one to study he says, "Why are you sitting there with books? Why do you just sit while I have to work to feed you? You should not be going to school. Your job is to get a husband, not to sit around with books, using up the candles."

I am lucky, though, because my mother stands up to him on this matter. She tells me to go to school, to study hard and make a good future for us.

My mother never had the chance to go to school. She cannot read or write. She has no experience of these things. But she knows how hard her life is, and she thinks that education might be the way to an easier life.

My great ambition is to one day work in a bank. It is a job that a woman can do where she will have good responsibility and where people will treat her with respect.

I cry sometimes because my uncle is very cruel to my mother and brother and me. He hits us. He says insulting things to us because he does not want to have us around, but we have nowhere else to go. When I get my job at the bank I will make a good salary and take us all to live in another place, far away from my uncle. But that is still many years from now.

We don't know what will make him angry. If we did, then we wouldn't do it. I think he is just angry when we breathe, and we can't do anything about that. My brother is a boy and can run outside, but my sisters and I can't just leave the house when we want to. It's not safe for us outside, either.

My uncle keeps threatening to find me a husband. I know that will be my fate, that one day he will marry me off to someone and I won't be able to disobey. But I hope I get to live part of my life for myself.

So I come to school a lot because school is a nicer place than home. After I finish regular classes I stay at school for special courses, like English, tailoring and computers. All classes are free at my school, as long as you do your work. You cannot just come and not work because someone else would make better use of your space.

When I do go home I spend most of my time taking care of my little brother and helping my mother wash clothes. My favorite food is spaghetti. Sometimes we have it here at school for lunch. I have one good friend, a girl in my class. She has a hard life, similar to mine, so we understand each other very well.

We both work hard in school. We hope one day to have a life.

Sharifa, 14

One of the legacies of decades-long war in Afghanistan has been the bombing, land-mining and burning of orchards and farmlands. Afghanistan used to grow enough food to feed itself. War changed that.

Farmers came back from war or exile to find that their land could not be used. But they still had families to feed. So they turned to a crop that can grow in rocky, dry soil — opium poppies.

Opium poppies produce a gummy substance that is the raw material for heroin, an illegal, addictive drug. The opium itself can be smoked. It is a painkiller, producing a heavy stoned feeling in those who smoke it.

Afghanistan now produces more than 90 percent of the world's heroin. It is used by addicts in Russia, Europe and North America. The trade is controlled by warlords and other criminals — and the Taliban — who have no interest in human rights or the well-being of children. The money they get from selling heroin buys them more guns and more power.

The poppy farmers are generally poor families growing poppies on small plots of land that will not support any other crops. They often have to borrow money to buy the seed. If their poppy crop is destroyed by foreign troops to prevent the heroin from being sold in their home countries, the farmers cannot repay the debt. So they may give in payment the only thing they have — a daughter. These girls who are forced into marriage — a form of rape and slavery — are called Opium Brides. Farmers who don't pay their debt have also been tortured and killed.

Heroin is a bad business.

In the absence of proper medicine, opium is used to get rid of pain, including the pain of hunger. Parents give it to babies who have earaches and to children whose bellies are empty. For adults, smoking opium eases the pain of long hours of back-breaking work, and it blocks out the memories of trauma from the war.

The number of opium addicts in Afghanistan is estimated at 1.5 million. In a country of thirty million

people, that works out to one of the highest rates of addiction of any country in the world. Treatment options are very few.

Anyone who has lived with or known an addict knows the kind of chaos and havoc they create around them.

Sharifa has an addicted father.

My brother is one year younger than me. We live with our mother. I hear from other girls how their family members sometimes argue, but we don't have that problem. The three of us have to pull together if we are to manage, and even then it is very hard. So we have no energy to waste in arguments. What would be the point? Our lives would still be hard, no matter who won the argument.

My mother washes clothes for neighbors and also does cooking jobs when she can, not as a formal cook but as a helper. My brother does odd jobs to help out, whatever he can, carrying things or helping someone out in their shops. He gets paid very little. He works hard, but people think he is young so they don't need to pay him much.

I wish there was a job I could do to earn money, but for Afghan girls it is very difficult.

My father is still alive, I think, but he does not live with us. As far as I know, he is in Karachi staying with relatives, but I can't be sure.

He is addicted to opium. He has been addicted for ten years. He used to be a shopkeeper. He kept up this job even while he was addicted, but then his health became too bad. He took more and more opium and he stopped working.

It was hard to live with him. Our house always smelled of opium smoke. My clothes, too, would hold the smell. When I went to school other children would call me names because of the smell on my clothes. I tried to keep clean but there was no place to hang clothes away from the smoke.

My father had many moods when he lived with us, all bad except when he had smoked a lot of opium. Then he just lay on the floor and didn't bother us. He had a lot of bad memories from the war, my mother said, and was in pain a lot of the time from injuries that had no proper treatment. Opium took away his pain and his memories.

When he didn't have opium, he would smoke hashish. When he could not get these things, then he would be in a very bad mood. He would yell and say bad things for hours and hours, mean and insulting things. We all lived in one room and there was no way to get away from the insulting things he said. And there was no way to make him feel better.

Finally, it got so bad my mother asked his relatives in Pakistan to take him in. I don't know how she came up with the money or how she got him to go. But he went away and now it is just the three of us.

I try to remember that my house is not me. Where we live it is very, very bad. We have no clean sheets, no beds. We sleep on the floor. We try to keep it clean but there is mud when it rains and dust when there is no rain.

We have no electricity, just a little oil lamp that we

light to do our homework, but we must work quickly and not waste the oil.

I like to have fun, and at school that can happen sometimes with my friends and classmates. We all work hard, but we can't be serious all the time! We are not old yet!

I have decided not to be married. I want to be a doctor, and I don't want a husband that I have to take care of. I want to do good work and make a better life for me and my family.

Sadaf, 12

One of the great Islamic traditions is the discipline of memorizing the entire Qur'an, the Islamic holy book. This tradition may spring from the days when books and literacy were less widespread than they are now. Memorizing and reciting the Qur'an was a way to pass on the words from one person to another.

A person who has accomplished this phenomenal task is called a hafiz. It is a revered title, one worthy of respect. The Qur'an is more than 86,000 words long, and it takes, on average, three to four years to memorize the whole thing. Anyone who has tried to memorize a poem for school will understand the concentration and dedication such a task takes! The children who accomplish this are said to be an extra special blessing to their parents.

Becoming a hafiz is a goal of Sadaf's.

I live with my mother and three sisters. My father was killed in a rocket attack a few years ago.

We were in our village, which has the name of Kolach. It was an ordinary place, not a special place.

My father liked to pray outside. He liked being under the sky instead of under a roof. So he was outside of the house, kneeling on his prayer mat, saying his prayers. And a rocket came down and killed him.

The rocket blew my whole house apart. There was nothing left of it. Maybe scraps of things. Nothing we could use. Nothing of value.

I was in my grandfather's house at the time, with my mother and sisters. My grandfather's house was right beside my house, so when the rocket hit my house, we felt it at Grandfather's.

It was very, very bad, so bad that you cannot even imagine it, like a nightmare. But worse than a nightmare. When you are next to a rocket exploding, you see it, you feel the ground shake, you hear the noise like a big animal roaring, and you smell it, too, the fire, the dust.

I did not want to believe that my father had been killed. I wanted to dig through the yard, through everything that was broken, to see if we could find him. But my grandfather took me away. It would not have helped. Of course he was dead.

I don't know who fired the rocket. Maybe it was the Taliban. Maybe it was the foreign soldiers. You think they would tell me? You think the Taliban would come to me and say, "Oh, we killed your father but we didn't mean to. The rocket went the wrong way." No, they don't do that. Nobody explains anything.

My father was a good man, a kind man. He liked his daughters to be smart and to learn things. He was proud when we learned how to read.

After the explosion my uncle took us away to another village to live with him. He is my mother's brother. We lived with him for a few years. My grandfather was too poor for us to stay with him. Now we are here in Kabul, trying to make a new life.

My two older sisters are married now, and they share everything with my mother and me. When they get some food, we get some food. My mother is jobless. She gets a bit of money from her brother, but not a lot. He is a laborer and does not make a lot of money.

The thing I most like to do is study the Qur'an. My father was killed while he was praying, and I think that makes his death holy in some way. I like to think so, anyway. By studying the Qur'an I feel that he is not so far away from me.

It is my dream to one day memorize all of the Qur'an. It was the wish of my father that all his girls be able to do this. I want to become a hafiz, which is what people will call me when I have memorized the whole Book of Allah.

It will be a big job. The Qur'an has 114 surahs [chapters] and over six thousand verses. But others have done it and I will be able to do it. Then the message of the Prophet will be inside me, and I'll always have it, even if all the Qur'ans disappear. And when I have a problem, I can know what part of the Holy Qur'an will help me solve it.

I haven't started to memorize it yet. I am still learning to read it, and I make a lot of mistakes. When I stop making mistakes, then I will start to memorize.

There is a television show on Afghan TV called Qur'an Star, for those who memorize the Qur'an, a kind of competition. I want to go on this program and do well. That is one good way I can help my family. The last winner was a sixteen-year-old girl. She won 150,000 afghanis ($3,000 US). My family will be helped a lot with that much money.

My mother says that when it is her turn to die, it will be my responsibility to recite the prayers over her body. She says that praying over her will be more important than crying over her, so I should practice the prayers and have them easy in my mind to get to when the time comes.

I hear that Kabul is a nice city, with parks and gardens and big shops and even a zoo, but I haven't seen any of that. All I have seen is this area, and it isn't very nice. It doesn't really matter, though, if you live in an ugly place. If you have beautiful thoughts in your head then it's like you are living in beauty.

In the future I want to be a teacher and teach both English and Islamic studies. People who know English are more respected, and if I am a scholar of Islamic studies, I can help spread the news of the Qur'an.

War comes when there is no unity, when people look out for themselves instead of each other. But through discussion we can solve all our problems, create unity and avoid war.

Mustala, 13

Life expectancy for people in Afghanistan is, on average, forty-four years. In Canada and the United States it is about eighty. Poor nutrition, lack of access to health care and clean water, exposure to the elements, poverty-related illnesses such as tuberculosis, plus war and related violence all take their toll. Twenty percent of all children born in Afghanistan die before they reach their fifth birthday.

Many people have fled Afghanistan because of the war. Others have left in search of jobs or a better life elsewhere.

In Canada and the United States, we have an economic safety net. People over sixty-five receive a pension. People who are out of work are often eligible for unemployment insurance. For those who are too ill to work, there is another type of assistance. We have these things because the people who came before us worked really hard to make them happen. We have also never suffered the horrible destruction of prolonged war on our land.

War creates poverty. In countries like Afghanistan, where there has been prolonged war, there is no economic safety net. People go hungry. According to UNICEF, nearly 40 percent of children under the age of five are undernourished, and over half of all children under five are smaller than they would be if they had enough to eat.

Mustala's family has been split apart by war.

I live with my grandfather and grandmother. We are really poor. My grandparents don't work. We have no money for soap, so I am often dirty and wearing dirty clothes. I would like to be better dressed, so when people see me coming they will think, "Oh, this boy is important, look at his clothes. He must be somebody special." No one will think that of me if I don't have nice clothes.

My father left when I was quite small. He went to Iran to find work and also because some people here wanted to kill him. My mother got another husband and left us so she could be with him. I think she has other children now.

I get free food at school, which is often the only time I

Classrooms and playground at Mustala's school.

eat, and sometimes my grandparents don't eat at all. When I can, I put food in my pockets at lunchtime to take back to my grandparents, but it is a thing that makes me nervous to do. I don't want to get in trouble. So, sometimes if I am hungry for two pieces of nan, I take two, but I don't eat them. I hide them in my jacket to take home. That's not stealing, is it?

This whole school is filled with kids who have a hard life but who are really smart, although not all are as smart as me or as good at playing football as me! Many have lost one parent or two parents in the war or from some illness. I have not lost my parents. They are both alive. They are just not with me.

I wish my father would come back from Iran, even for a day. He would see what a smart, good boy I've become, and he would keep me with him. I don't care where. I could go back to Iran with him or we could stay here. Or we could go someplace else. I would be fine with any decision.

Sometimes my mother sends my grandparents a little bit of money to help out. This way I know she hasn't forgotten about me. Her new husband would not want me to live with him, so I don't think about that or dream about that. When I get to be a man, maybe I can take care of my mother and she won't have to live with him anymore. But that's a long way off.

I was young when my father left, maybe five or six. Sometimes, when I'm playing football with my friends, a man will stop and watch us or will walk by really slowly, and I think, "Maybe that's my father." I play extra well then, so that he'll take me away with him. He won't want a son who is no good at football.

It gets very dark in our house at night, and sometimes I get afraid. When you hear things in the dark and you can't see what they are, anybody would be afraid. It doesn't mean I'm not brave. But if someone shoots a gun or there is yelling or a cat screams, it can get scary. When I get scared I try to think of football or I practice my English.

I think Afghanistan could be a great country, especially if I was the president. I'd help all the poor people and make sure they have food and electric light. I would make a law that everybody has to go to school. Even adults, because there are a lot of adults who have never been to school, and I think that makes them have bad tempers. If they see me going to school, they yell at me that I should be working. So I would make them to go school, too, so that they'd stop bothering me.

We need to study to make a good country out of Afghanistan. Right now we are a backwater country. At school I have learned there are better ways to do things than all this war, war, war all the time. It's the young generation that will change that.

My generation.

Me.

Ajmal, 11

In the western part of Kabul is a holiday spot called Qargha Lake. It has guesthouses that are rented by Kabul's elite during the summer, a beach with donkey rides for kids, a picnic area, a restaurant and even an old amusement park. Nearby is the golf course that was built by King Habibullah in 1911, occupied by Soviet tanks during the 1980s, and then planted with land mines by the Taliban. When the Taliban left, it became a place where people were trained in how to remove land mines, and now golf is played there again.

Ajmal and his younger sister, Spegmai, try to get

My sister is ten. We live in a neighborhood a little ways from here. It takes us a while to walk here. I don't know how long. I don't carry a clock. A while.

Both my sister and I go to school, but we don't go every day. Sometimes the school is closed. Sometimes it is open and we go but the teacher doesn't show up, so we leave again. Sometimes there is no food or money in our house so we have to go out to work instead of going to school.

Our mother is dead. I don't know how she died. She was sick, I think, and we had no medicine. So she died.

Our father is also sick, but he is not dead. His sickness is in his legs. When he is feeling well he looks through garbage to find something we can eat or use. He taught us how to do that, and so we do it when we are out.

You have to pay attention. You can't just go walk and think of other things. You have to see everything and think about if what you see is useful. I found a plastic bag on the beach this morning and put it in my pocket. A plastic bag is useful.

Today it is cold and the lake is frozen. Not many people are here, so we don't make much money. When there are a lot of cars we stand in the street and bang on their windows.

Our work is to ask people for money, and when they give us money we burn some coal and the smoke takes away the evil spirits. We make maybe 35 afghanis a day (about 75 cents) when people are kind.

Qargha Lake holiday spot.

My sister likes this work more than I do. She is better at running than me, and she is pretty and speaks well, so people are nicer to her.

I do not run well. My legs have a kind of sickness like my father's, and you can see I do not speak well. So people laugh at me and call me names.

If people don't want to give us money, that's okay. They don't have to. We are small. What can we do to them if they don't give? But why do they have to be mean? Why do they have to call us dogs and say bad words? That's what I do not like about this job.

My sister likes writing the best in school and I like reading the best. I would like to become something in the future. I don't know what, just somebody of importance. Maybe I'll become a teacher. When I'm a teacher I will show up for work every day so my students don't waste time sitting in an empty classroom with nothing to learn.

Amullah, 15

Cricket was made popular by Afghans who had spent time as refugees in Pakistan, where cricket is played and followed with great enthusiasm.

When the Taliban came to power in 1996, they banned the game. They allowed Afghanistan's national cricket team to play again in 2000, but spectators were not allowed to cheer or clap. All they could do to show their enthusiasm was say "Allahu Akbar," which means God Is Great. And the games had to be scheduled around the executions and torture that the Taliban carried out in that same stadium.

Amullah and his friends are taking advantage

of a free day to work on their cricket game in the schoolyard.

My father is a farmer, or he used to be. We had to leave our land when I was small because of the war. There was shooting, bombing, people being killed for no reason. I don't remember much about that time because I was very small, but my older brothers have told me. It got so bad that we couldn't stay there. We moved around a lot, from place to place, trying to find somewhere safe. We ended up in Kabul.

My father now works as a shopkeeper in someone else's shop.

I don't remember much about the Taliban time. Like I said, I was really small. My brothers said that for them, the worst thing was that they couldn't play sports. The Taliban wouldn't let them. They wouldn't let anybody play. But people would listen to games from India and Pakistan on radios they kept secret.

How could they say, "No more football, no more cricket"? Those are the best things in life! It's a good thing I was small. If they came back into the government with those rules, I would go mad. I remember my brothers trying to play football and cricket in our house, but we had a very small house, and our mother did not like them playing ball inside.

My school is on holiday today, but we all came here to practice because we have a big cricket match coming up soon against another school, and of course we want to win!

Cricket practice at Amullah's school.

All of us, yes, we like to play, but we also want to do good things for Afghanistan, like be teachers, doctors, engineers — all of the best kind because there is so much to do.

I want to finish my schooling here, then go on to study agriculture. My father talks about his little farm, how much he loved it, and I would like to get that back for him. Probably not the same farm. That's all gone in the war, but another piece of land, a better piece. Then I would take him and my mother out of Kabul to a place that is cleaner and quieter, and they can have some peace.

I think it is good to study agriculture because there are new ways of doing everything. All the time, people are coming up with new ideas. Some may not be good, but some may be very good. So I'll learn all I can, then become a good farmer. Maybe even a rich one!

But first we need better security. Everyone is tired of being afraid. Here in the schoolyard everyone is playing hard and we're having fun, but we can never really forget about the security. We see helicopters every day and military cars and trucks, and things still get blown up.

But if all that can stop, then Afghanistan will be great, because there are so many of us who want it to be great, it can't be anything else.

Shabona, 14

Years of war and repression have left Afghanistan lacking many basic things that other countries take for granted. A country without a fully functioning education system, for instance, cannot hope to move forward. After the fall of the Taliban, Afghanistan needed everything — school buildings, books, chalk, pens and teachers. Trained teachers were in short supply. The Soviets, the warlords during the civil war and the Taliban all targeted teachers because teachers have such power to encourage independent thought — and independent thought is the enemy of despots.

Teacher training is a priority for many organizations working to help rebuild Afghanistan — especially training women, since many families don't want their daughters to be taught by male teachers.

At a large wedding hall in Kabul, teachers from all over the area have gathered to learn new teaching methods from each other. Shabona and her classmates are taking part.

We are from a high school about an hour from the city of Kabul. We have come here today to sing for the teachers who are part of this teacher-training conference. We sang the Afghan national anthem this morning and we'll sing something else this afternoon.

I like the national anthem. It lists all the tribes in Afghanistan, and it's about how everyone should work together, even though they don't.

Then we had to sit and listen to the teachers. Some of them talked too much, but some were interesting.

Some teachers sat up front in rows and pretended to be students while other teachers took turns pretending to teach math or science and other subjects in new ways to make it a better experience for the students. Some of their ideas would work better than others, in my opinion. I think it's better to have a conversation with your students, not just talk all the time, because that can make us drift off, especially if we're hungry.

Our school is a good school, but there is no safe place for us to run around outside. We are girls but we want to move, too! It would be nice to have some green space that is safe so we could run around without being stared at or yelled at.

I like most to study science. At my school we can study geometry, math, chemistry and biology. It's all from books and sheets of paper and notes on the blackboard. We have two microscopes but they are very old and broken.

There are so many girls who want to come to our school. We have almost 2,500 girls! We have to go to school in shifts. I'm on the morning shift. I'd like to go to school all day but we have to make room for the others.

I was really young when the Taliban were in power, so I don't remember a whole lot. Our teacher remembers. Whenever she thinks we are not studying hard enough, she tells us about that time. She had to leave school and was stuck at home most of the time. Her aunt had a little school for girls in her home. Not a school, just a study group, really, but it had to be very secret. Our teacher would put her schoolbooks in a basket, then cover them up with fruit so the Taliban wouldn't find out that she was studying.

The Taliban were ignorant. They didn't know that men and women are equals. It says so in the Qur'an.

The Taliban broke their own rules all the time, too. Our teacher's brother was arrested by them three times. He had a little shop, a secret shop that sold satellite dishes for televisions. These were against the law, so the Taliban would arrest him. But then they would say, "You can go free if you give me a satellite dish."

Our teacher says it was hard for her to go back to school after the Taliban because her brain wasn't used to working.

She says if studying hard becomes a habit with us, then we'll be able to continue the habit if we are ever forced out of school again.

We joke around, but we are also serious students. We want to be doctors or journalists or members of parliament or teachers. We will have to get there through hard work because none of our families have money. Just in this group we have girls whose fathers died in the war, who have had family members injured or homes that were blown up.

I was living in an area south of Kabul. There was a lot of war there, even after the Taliban were kicked out of power. We had lots of rockets, lots of shooting, lots of explosions. It was very scary. I remember not wanting to leave my mother's side. She would even just go into the next room and I'd scream because I was afraid I would never see her again.

We were about to go to Kabul where it was supposed to be safer. Really, we were ready to go, about to get into the car, when a rocket hit the car and it exploded. So we were stuck until we could find another car to take us.

For fun, my friends and I try on each other's makeup and try out each other's cellphones. We would really like a place to exercise and play sports, but we have nothing like that. We do it in a small way, inside, but it would be great to be able to just run and run and run.

Will there be another war? We hope not! Afghanistan has had too much war. If war has to happen, let it happen somewhere else. Do you have war in Canada? Maybe it is your turn, then.

Abdul, 14, and Noorina, 15

Scouting has a long tradition in Afghanistan, as it does in many countries. In 1978 it was banned by the Communists, who wanted to set up their own youth organizations. It stayed banned during the civil war and the Taliban regime. In 2003 it was started up again with the help of international donors, and now it is sponsored by the ministry of education. Afghan Scouts perform a variety of public services, from cleaning mosques to assisting firefighters.

Abdul and Noorina are very proud of what they are accomplishing in their Scout troop.

Abdul — Everyone in this Scout troop has lost at least one parent. We have come from many different provinces — Laghman, Kandahar, Daikundi, Lowgar, Badakhshan — all over. We live in a special place called Maristoon on the edge of Kabul.

Maristoon means community in Dari. The people who live here all have some special struggles. They are orphans or they are disabled, and everyone is very poor. But even with all that, we can do many things.

My own father is dead. My mother is blind. I'm not sure how she became blind. I think it was in the war. The war killed my father. My mother won't tell me much about it.

Noorina — My father used to work at the Afghan Embassy in Moscow, under a different time. Our whole life has been back and forth from war to war. When things were dangerous for us in Afghanistan, we went to Quetta in Pakistan and lived in a refugee camp. Then when Karzai became president, my father thought Afghanistan would be safe so we went home. But it was not good. It was still dangerous. So we went back to Pakistan.

My father set up a little shop in Pakistan. Just a little place selling groceries and little things. One day he went out to the shop very early, without even having breakfast. So my mother and I decided to take him breakfast. We got some food together but when we got to the shop, there was no shop! A rocket had hit it. The whole thing blew up. But my father wasn't killed in the explosion. Someone shot him. So maybe he got out of the shop when he heard the rocket coming and thought, "Oh, good, I'm safe." Then someone came along and shot him. I don't know if that's how it happened or not. I just imagine it like that.

It wasn't safe for us in Pakistan. So we came back to Afghanistan. I hope it will be safe this time.

Abdul — We all have stories like that. Nazifa's father was kidnapped by the Taliban and then killed three days later. Naramullah's father was shot. Aziz lost both of his parents in the war. He lived with his uncle, a doctor who treated people in the refugee camps around Kandahar. His uncle died of a heart attack. Lots of stories. It's normal for us.

We belong to Scouts because it is a way to improve ourselves and improve our community. It is part of the Scout promise:

On my honor I promise to Allah that I will do my
   best
To do my duty to Allah, and my country Afghanistan
To help other people at all times
And to obey the Scout law.

We learn a lot in Scouts. Seeking knowledge is our whole mission. We learn how to respect elders, how to keep the environment clean, how to prevent fires. We live in a green area — well, it will be green when the spring comes. We learn how to take care of trees and land. Afghanistan has been through a lot. A lot of the country has been destroyed, but we can make it beautiful again.

I have both good and bad memories of the Taliban.

Mostly they were very bad, but sometimes they would bring food to families who needed it. They helped my family in this way, so this is a good memory.

We see a lot of foreign troops. Scouting is a normal thing in many parts of the world. It was started by a British man in 1907. When the foreign troops hear about our Scout troop they want to come and visit us. Just last week some foreign soldiers came and took us on a hike into the hills behind Maristoon. That was a good day although not for our Scout leader. She had a hard time keeping up!

There are boys and girls together in this Scout troop. Men and women will have to work together to rebuild the country, so we learn here to be leaders. Good leaders. Leaders that people will trust. Afghanistan needs that.

Fareeba, 12

In wealthy countries, people with mental illness have a rough time, even when they are supported with resources, pensions, medication and therapy. In poor countries, people with mental illness are often at the bottom of the pile.

War creates trauma, and trauma can lead to mental illness. In 2010, the Afghan government estimated that two-thirds of the Afghan people suffer from psychological problems such as depression, severe anxiety and post-traumatic stress disorder. Treatment options are limited, with fewer than fifty psychologists and psychiatrists in the whole country.

Without good medical alternatives, people sometimes turn to tradition and superstition. These include dropping off their loved one at a shrine. There, patients are suspected of being possessed by demons, or djinns. The patients are fed only bread and water and are kept in chains in small cement rooms. They stay this way for forty days, which is supposed to drive away the demon. The World Health Organization has started a Chain Free Initiative to try to provide medications that might be more beneficial than superstition.

Fareeba is twelve years old — maybe. She comes from Mazar-e-Sharif — maybe. She was found wandering in the streets and was brought to the mental hospital by strangers — also maybe.

Fareeba lives behind the high stone walls of the women's mental hospital. She was dropped off at the metal gate by two people who may have been her parents but denied kinship. There is a huge stigma against people with mental illness in Afghanistan, as there is everywhere else.

Behind the walls of the women's mental hospital, there is sunshine. The women patients are allowed to roam the grounds freely during the day. The walls keep them safe from outsiders who might want to hurt them.

Recently a volunteer from another country helped the patients plant gardens and taught them to care for the plants. Even though it is winter now and nothing is growing, two women are digging in the dirt because that is an activity they enjoy. Others sit and enjoy the sun on their faces. Others follow me around and stare in curiosity at such a funny-looking visitor.

Fareeba cannot speak. She might be able to if she had a therapist to work with her, but there is no one. Judging from her hand gestures and the way she behaves, Fareeba may have autism, but there is no way to have her properly diagnosed, and no one is trained to give her the specialized therapy she requires. There is no next step for her, no place for her to progress to. She is just here, perhaps for the rest of her life.

In many ways, Fareeba is lucky. She is in a place where she and the other patients — all adult women — are kept clean. She has a bed to sleep in with a blanket (unless she makes too much noise at night; then she is put into the room with the big cages, locked away from the others). She is fed every day, and she can go out into the yard at her own whim. The staff are compassionate and competent. No one is being mean to her.

But she has never been to school, never seen a speech therapist, never been given toys and tasks that might help her move forward. Her future is more of the present. This is her life.

Shyah, 14

As different Afghan governments persecuted people with education, trained professionals like doctors and nurses fled the country to save their lives. Under the Taliban, women could not be treated by male doctors, and female doctors were not allowed to work. People who became injured often stayed injured.

A broken leg that is not repaired does not mend on its own. Physical injuries that are not properly treated can lead to long-term difficulties.

SOLA is an organization that tries to repair some of the damage that war and the resulting poverty have caused. It arranges rehabilitative surgery in the United States for kids like Shyah, who are given a home and an education so that when their bodies are repaired, they are better equipped to make something of their lives.

I am from Shamoli, in Parwan Province. I have been at this school for two years, without my family. My mother is dead. She died soon after I was born. My father remarried, and his new wife did not take care of me very well.

I can't say she didn't like me. I was a baby. I had no personality to like or dislike. Maybe she didn't like babies. Whatever it was, she didn't take good care of me.

I was six months old when my legs went all wrong. Someone in my family put me up on a high stack of mattresses and pillows. It was very high and I fell off. My legs got broken and twisted, but there was no treatment, no hospitals or clinics, so they did not heal.

With my legs in bad shape, I guess I was even harder to care for and even more of a problem for my stepmother, so my father did the best thing he knew what to do for me. He put me in an orphanage. That's where I grew up.

It was okay there. It wasn't a huge orphanage, just a medium one, and I think that's better than a really big one. You could get lost in too many kids. When I got old enough I went to school for two hours in the morning, then had lunch, then I went to the mosque in the afternoon for religious studies. It was my life. It was what I knew.

Two years ago some people came to the orphanage looking for kids like me who needed help, and so I came to this school.

This is part home, where I live, part school and part waiting room. All the kids here are waiting to go to other countries for medical treatment, or they have been accepted into foreign universities and they are waiting for their visas to come through.

I have been to the United States once for surgery, and I'm waiting to go again for another operation on my legs. I was sent to Charlotte, North Carolina. I was very happy there. The people in the hospital were very kind to me — so kind that I wasn't even afraid.

When I came out of the hospital I stayed with an American family to get my strength back. They were great. They had two sons and we all played together. It didn't matter that they were American and I was Afghan. We played board games, computer games, video games, we went into the city to swim or see a movie. I liked it a lot.

When I was younger I was not interested in studying. My mother was dead and when my father came to see me, he didn't encourage me. He never went to school. I don't think he thought I could ever do anything, that my legs were bad and that would be my whole life. I would grow up to be the man with bad legs.

But since coming to SOLA, all that has changed for me. Studying is a very important activity here. All the kids are expected to take it seriously. I am the youngest student here. All the other kids think they can check up on me. "Have you done your homework?" "Don't you have a test to study for?" There is no chance not to study! So now I am a very good student. My favorite things to study are English and the Qur'an.

There are two kinds of students who live here. Some are like me, waiting to go for medical treatment.

Najib is my friend. He is from Helmand Province. He is a little older than me. On election day two years ago he took his little brother into town on a bicycle. A rocket came. There was an explosion and a tiny piece of shrapnel went into his eye. The rocket killed his little brother.

Najib had one operation but he needs another. It is all

arranged for him to go to the United States but now he is waiting for the visa.

When he was in Helmand, he worked for a mechanic and thought he would always work for a mechanic. Now, after meeting more people and learning more things, he wants to be an eye doctor. He gets great grades in sciences like biology and chemistry.

The other students have been granted scholarships to foreign universities. They are waiting for visas, too. The visa officers who work at the embassy are sometimes not helpful. One girl was all set to go away to college, but during her visa interview the officer told her, "How can you go to college when you haven't been to high school?" But in Afghanistan, school is not regular. She has been tutored and passed the university entrance exam. But the visa officer did not understand that and denied her visa. Another girl was told, "You already have a high school education, you don't need more than that." And her visa was denied.

But maybe everyone's visas will come through soon, and then we'll go on to the next step for our futures. We are not really family in this school but we feel like family. We are from all over Afghanistan, but it's like we are all brothers and sisters. Family.

Zuhal, 13

The Kabul Women's Garden is a special place. In a society where women are not allowed to wander freely, to go outside to stretch their legs when they feel like some fresh air — because either the laws prevent it or customs make it very difficult — the garden gives them a place to walk, unharassed by men.

The eight acres were donated by King Zahir Shah in the 1940s. Not surprisingly, the Taliban closed the garden when they took over. They filled it with garbage and changed its name from Women's Garden to Spring Garden. Only men went there, to attend the rooster fights that took place in the middle of the rubble.

After the fall of the Taliban, Afghan women, supported by international donations, reclaimed the garden, even doing much of the manual labor required to make it beautiful again — a rare thing in Afghanistan, where the idea of women working in the trades has not really taken hold. Forty-five truckloads of trash were carried away, five thousand rose bushes were planted and all sorts of trees were added.

The Women's Garden reopened on November 3, 2010. It is a little spot of paradise in the middle of a noisy, busy city. There are pathways, fountains, gazebos and children's playgrounds. Women can exercise in the fitness center and on the basketball court, enjoy lunch at the restaurant and study at the computer lab or take job training. They can take a tae kwon do class, shop at the small boutiques, or just sit and have quiet for a few minutes.

The garden also has a mosque, built and maintained by women, where women can receive religious instruction from other women.

It is a safe place. The garden has high walls around it and one gate guarded by a male armed guard. After visitors pass through the gate, one of the female intelligence officers checks in bags and under burqas to make sure a suicide bomber or assassin hasn't slipped through.

Zuhal and her friend have come to the garden to play.

My mother works at home, taking care of us. My father has a job with the government.

I am very good at school. I'm in grade eight and I get lots of praise from my teachers because I work hard and learn fast. My favorite subject to study is English because if you know English, you can get a good job.

But today is a day when there are no classes. I have come here with my friend to the Women's Garden. My mother came with us, but she has gone inside to a literacy class and we have stayed outside to play. I like it here because only girls are allowed. It's a place where I can relax.

The garden has a high wall around it that keeps out the noise and dirt of the city. When I am on this side of the wall, I can pretend the whole world is pretty and safe.

The security here is very good. There is a guard out front and you have to be a woman or a girl to get past him. Then there are other guards, women, inside the gate who search everyone's bag to make sure no one is bringing a bomb into the garden. I don't know why anyone would want to blow up a garden, but people do strange things. Once that's over, you can just come into the garden and feel free.

Outside the walls there is a lot of noise from all the cars and trucks on the road. There is a lot of dust and dirt and it is hard to breathe.

Here in the garden, things are different. The walls block out the noise. I know that dust and noise travel, but they don't seem to come in here. The garden is clean. The air is easier to breathe.

I don't feel free outside the garden. Neither does my

A rainy day in the Women's Garden.

friend. It's because of men that we don't feel free. We feel they are watching us and judging us. They haven't said anything directly to me or tried to bother me, but my mother tells me to be careful around them, and not to relax out there. She remembers living under the Taliban, when all men were cruel to women, not just the Taliban. She said the Taliban told men that women were bad and a lot of men believed them, and they would treat women badly even if they weren't part of the Taliban. I try to tell her that things have changed, but she always says, "Things haven't changed that much!"

So we're careful when we are out in the world, but behind these walls, in this garden, we don't have to be careful. We can play and laugh and there is no one to frown at us.

Sometimes my friend and I like to play on the swings, like we're doing today. Sometimes we run around on all the pathways until we are breathing really hard and we can feel our hearts pounding. Sometimes we feel like being quiet and we just sit on a bench. There are shops as you just come into the garden. Did you see them? They sell dresses and things for hair and for babies. Sometimes we look in the shops or buy a treat from the tea house.

Outside the walls there are a lot of soldiers in the streets. You see them on tanks or army trucks and they carry big machine guns. Some are foreign soldiers, some are Afghan. I am not afraid of them. It's what I have always seen, ever since I can remember. They don't bother me because I don't make trouble for anyone.

I don't know what I want for the future. That's a long way off! I guess I want good security and a nice life and a good education. But right now, I just want to swing with my friend.

Parwais, 17

Because of its location, Afghanistan has been at the crossroads for many armies and civilizations. Coins have been found there from ancient Greece and Persia, artifacts from Mongolia and statues from ancient Buddhist societies.

The National Museum of Afghanistan used to hold the most complete record of Central Asian history anywhere in the world, dating all the way back to prehistoric times. But it, too, fell victim to the war.

When the Soviets occupied Afghanistan, Kabul was relatively safe from bombing. A lot of Soviets were stationed there, and they protected the city to protect themselves. When the Soviets left, civil war broke out as the different groups that had been fighting the Soviets turned their guns on each other — each wanted to be the boss of Afghanistan. Bombs started falling on the capital city.

The museum was bombed in 1993, destroying the top floor and leaving it open to looters, who sold the treasures to private collectors all around the world. Although attempts were made to secure the rest of the collection by bolting the doors and bricking up the windows, the looting continued. Most of the collection disappeared.

Then, in March 2001, the Taliban decided to destroy many statues and art objects, including the few that had managed to survive in the museum.

Since the fall of the Taliban, a lot of effort has gone into rebuilding the museum and bringing back as much of the collection as possible. A country's history — and the things that tell of its history — reminds its people that their present is built on something, and that they are building toward the future.

Parwais is originally from Bagram, north of Kabul. He now works at the National Museum as a cleaner.

We left Bagram during the Taliban. They were very hard to the people there, very bad. So much war, guns, shooting, killing. They killed my father. They burned so many houses and shops. I don't know why they did these things. Just because they could. No one could stop them.

My older brother took charge of the family after my father was killed. He asked around about where it might be safer and decided to bring us all to Kabul so that we might have some kind of life.

I have never attended school. No one in my family has. It's just not something we have had the chance to do. I don't know if I would want to go or not. I don't know what it means to go.

Even though I never went to school, I am still able to have a good job. I work at the Kabul museum. It is my job to clean the floors and the staircases and anything else that has to be cleaned. It is a very good job because it is inside, so even if the weather is bad, I am warm and dry. The work is not hard and the museum is quiet. Some people spend all their time lifting heavy things or carrying things through traffic, and their back hurts and they get dirty and there is always noise. So this is a very good job.

My cousin had this job before me. When he left it for another job, he suggested that I take over from him. The museum bosses said yes, and now I work hard so they will keep me on.

The best thing about this job is that I get to look at all the exhibits. We have a lot of very old objects here in this museum. Most got broken or even destroyed in the war. Some things were stolen. Some of the things that were lost were found again but they were broken, and if you look at them closely you can see where they were put back together.

The displays have cards next to them that explain what they are. I can't read the cards — that's one thing I would like to go to school to learn — but the people who work here explain things to me and I hear them talking to each other. I learn from listening, and it is very interesting.

I didn't know Afghanistan was so old. I guess I never thought about it until I started working here. Who can spend time thinking about things like that on a regular day? There is too much work to do. But here, I get to think about it all the time. So many people lived here before I did, and their lives were a little bit like mine and they were also different.

I have two favorite things in this museum. One is a statue of a bird that has an oil burner inside. I like to look at it and think about who made it. Why did he think to do such a thing? What made him think it was a good idea? Did the maker use it himself or did he give it to someone else to use?

My most favorite thing is a large bowl made out of clay. It is very old and the colors on it are not fancy but I think they are beautiful. When I look at it I imagine it full of food, and a family is sitting around it having a meal together. Maybe the family that used it hundreds of years ago was not very different from my family.

These are the kinds of things I like to think about when I am doing my cleaning.

The future of Afghanistan? I hope everyone gets a chance to study. Some of us, like me, did not get that chance, but I think it would be better if everyone went to school. There is a lot I don't know, and the country will be stronger if it is run and helped by people who know things.

The future for me? Well, I just hope I can work here at the museum for a long, long time.

Palwasha, 16

During the reign of the Taliban, the soccer stadium was a torture chamber. Every Friday they would force spectators into the seats to watch prisoners being punished. People were beaten. They had arms cut off. Some were shot in the back of the head or had their heads cut off. Others were strung up on the gallows. Terrible things happened in that stadium.

Today it is a place where the Afghan Women's National Football Team has their offices. Palwasha is a member of that team. Sometimes they practice in the old soccer stadium. Today they are practicing on a field at the headquarters of NATO in Kabul.

I love football. I play on the national women's football team and I am also trained as a referee. I play defense. I love to run.

When I'm not playing football, I'm attending computer science classes at the university.

I went to Pakistan during the Taliban time. My uncle took me. We were there for many years. I was able to go to school and to play football, so when I came back to Afghanistan I had not lost too much time. My parents stayed back in Afghanistan, so I didn't see them for years. I missed them terribly, and they missed me. But they wanted me to keep up with my studies, and they knew I loved to play sports. That's why they sent me away to another country for so long.

The Taliban were against all things for women and girls. No school, no sports, no music, no jobs. Nothing, like we were not even human. Some of that feeling is still around in Afghanistan. Some people think that girls should not play sports, although the boys I know do not think that. If they did, I don't think they would dare say so to me!

It is still hard to be a girl in Afghanistan. The laws are really good, but not everyone pays attention to the law. As girls we cannot just go out for a walk on our own. We cannot do what we want to do the way girls in other countries can. It is not safe. So girls are not free. Some of the girls who play on the team have to argue with their families to let them play — not because their families don't think girls should play, but they are worried about their safety.

Some Afghan people have closed minds. They think

Practice day for the Afghan Women's National Football Team.

women should only do certain jobs, that women should not run around because it is immodest. These are all old ideas. I think they will disappear one day, but it will take some time.

We are not paid to be on the team, and many of the girls have families with very little money. It is hard for them to afford the transportation to come to practice, especially since a lot of them live far away, across the city.

We have no regular, safe place to practice. Today we are playing on a field at ISAF (International Security Assistance Force) headquarters. The area is surrounded by tanks and soldiers from America and other places. The field isn't a real football field. It's rough and hard to run on, and at least once every time we practice, a military helicopter lands on the field.

Sometimes we have to practice on the men's basketball court. The men have a regular field to practice on. We would like to have a safe place, too.

Sometimes we play on the big field at the stadium, the same stadium the Taliban used for all the terrible things they did — the shootings, cutting off people's hands, the executions and torture. When we play there, when we run fast and play hard and when people — women and men — cheer us on, it is like we are getting some justice for all those women who were hurt. We play for them as much as ourselves.

We are a very good team and we have been invited to play against other teams in other countries. I have played in Germany, both in Berlin and in Frankfurt. I've played in Jordan, in Pakistan and in Bangladesh.

But there are powerful groups in Afghanistan who are always looking for things to use against us. They are part of the old way of thinking I was telling you about. That thinking will end, but it is still around. So I don't know if we will make it to Canada or not.

My hope for Afghanistan is that all girls will be able to play football, basketball, volleyball, track, or whatever other sport they enjoy. We are free when we are playing sports, and girls need to be free.

My hope for myself is to become the best referee in Afghanistan.

We have to be brave and strong and stand up for our rights, and not let anyone take us down.

Noorahu, 16

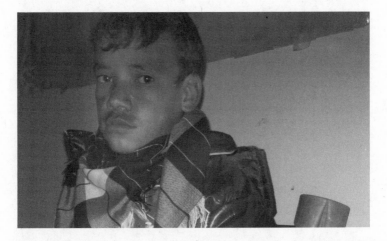

Afghanistan is one of the most heavily land-mined countries on Earth. A land mine is a cheap weapon. It can be easily put in the ground, and whoever walks on it will lose a limb or their eyes or their life. Many of the armies that have trampled on Afghanistan since the 1970s have put down land mines. But they didn't pick them up again. The mines stayed in the ground and kept on killing long after the war was declared over and the armies went home.

The Afghan Landmine Survivors' Organization (ALSO) supports victims of land mines through education, rehabilitation and job training. An important aspect of their work is struggling against the stigma faced by people with disabilities. Parents, not knowing what to do, will sometimes neglect their disabled children, and the city is not accessible, so disabled people have a hard time getting around.

One of the ways ALSO fights against the stigma is to run a community center in a very poor neighborhood that holds classes and brings together students of all ages, with and without disabilities.

The center is in a small rundown building a short way down an alley off a busy street. It is one room with torn plaster walls, divided up into classrooms by boards and sheets of plastic. The classrooms are crowded with kids sitting on the floor and looking up at chalkboards.

Noorahu is a student at this center. His legs were damaged by a land mine.

Some of the children at this center are like me. They have bad legs or no legs or a hand missing or something wrong like that. Other students have everything they are supposed to have. We are all treated the same. When a teacher is talking you can't tell if they are talking to a disabled kid or a regular kid. So no one feels different.

This is the first time I've gone to classes. It has been too hard to go to school before this. Before this community center opened up, the nearest school was very far away.

It is hard for me to walk with my legs damaged. I have crutches to help me, but it is still hard and it hurts. There is no money in my family for me to take taxis to school, so I haven't been able to go to a regular school.

My father doesn't work every day. He is a cook, and he helps prepare meals for wedding parties. When there is no wedding, he does not work, so there is very little money in our house. Sometimes when he cooks for a wedding, there is food left over, and the family who has hired him lets him take some food home to us. We eat very well on those nights because my father is a very good cook.

Outside of this center, people say negative things to me because of my disability. They call me names. They say things that make me feel not good about myself. When there are a lot of younger boys and they make fun of me, it is very hard for me to get away from them. They can run and jump around me and try to knock me down, and when I fall, they just laugh. I can't get away from them when they come at me because my legs are damaged. My legs won't move fast.

It's not just small children who act bad this way. Sometimes grown men say bad things to me, like I am bad luck and I am moving too slow. Not all adults are like this. Many are kind and they help me up if I fall. But some are not nice.

In this place, everyone is nice to me. Even kids who are not disabled. They treat me like I am normal.

Our teacher was hurt by a land mine when she was a child. She was thirteen when it happened. Her family had just finished a meal, and she had to do the dishes. She walked to the back of the house where the dishwashing area was and she stepped on a land mine. Some army had put land mines in her house. She stepped on a land mine, and the next thing she knew she was waking up in the hospital and her leg was gone.

She is a good teacher. When she teaches us we don't see that she has a leg missing. If she can become a teacher with no leg, maybe I can do something important, too.

Here I have friends, and I never had friends before. My good friend is Mosan. His father was killed by the Taliban. His mother makes carpets at home, and he thought his whole life would be making carpets, too. Then he started lessons here, and now he has bigger dreams.

We both want to be artists, which we can do whether we have legs or not. This center is big on art. Many kids like to draw, and the teachers put our best work up on the walls to encourage us.

I like to draw nature. Mostly what I have seen in my life has not been pretty. We live in a very poor area of Kabul. It is not beautiful. But I have seen photos at this center of beautiful natural places in the world. And even in the ugly parts of Kabul, flowers bloom. You just have to take the time to look for them.

Angela, 17

One of the ways people from different nations get beyond thinking of other nationalities in stereotypes is by meeting each other and getting to know each other as individuals.

The Youth Exchange and Study Program (YES) was set up in 2004 by the US State Department to give Afghan kids the chance for a first-class education and to get to know Americans as ordinary people, beyond the soldiers they see in Afghanistan.

Angela spent a year in the United States going to high school as part of the YES program. She is now such an accomplished English speaker that she has been hired several times to do short-term translation jobs for foreigners, including myself!

Meanwhile, the YES program was suspended in 2011 after many of the students fled the United States to become refugees in Canada rather than return to Afghanistan

I am originally from a village in Bamiyan. My parents are still there.

I was very young when the Taliban were in power. The war in Bamiyan was really bad. The Taliban were fighting an army called Hezbe-Watan, an army of Hazara people. The Taliban hated Hazara people. They killed so many people in Bamiyan. If they saw men or boys on the street, they would just shoot them dead, right in the street.

My family was in danger like everybody else in the country. The men, especially, were in danger. We all went up into the mountains with my uncle and his family. First we tried hiding the men in a basement room, but we were afraid that the Taliban would not believe us if they came and we told them the men were all dead. Plus, women alone could not go out of their homes and we were running out of food. So that could not last. So we went up into the mountains.

Remember, I was very young. I was not too bothered by the trip to the mountains because my mother was with me and I knew she would take care of me. I knew that the journey was hard. We left in a hurry, when the Taliban were patrolling another neighborhood, so there was no time to pack what we needed. And we didn't have much anyway. No water, almost no food. It was very cold and uncomfortable. We had no house in the mountains, no tent. We just slept on the rocks and tried to stay out of the wind. I was young, so they protected me as much as they could, but I knew that we were in a bad condition.

I don't know how long we stayed in the mountains. Weeks, I think. We ran out of food very early. I remember being cold and hungry and bored and scared. My brother and uncle tried to return to the village to get us food and blankets, but the Taliban were all over the place. There was a lot of killing going on. So they returned to the mountains with empty hands.

We were all so cold and so hungry that it was decided that the women and children would return home and the men and teenaged boys would stay in the mountains. The women would try to get food to the men. I remember the journey back down the mountains. It was not good.

We were home for three days. It was bad.

My brother loved books. He was a good student and had a lot of books. The Taliban were against books and they would arrest people who had them. So the first thing my mother did when we got back home was she burned all my brother's books and then she threw the ashes away far from our house. We had a cassette player, too, and some music cassettes. We buried these in the yard because they were also against the law.

My father was worried about us and came down the mountain to check on us. The Taliban arrested him.

The Taliban really hated the Hazaras, but they also

didn't like Tajiks. My mother is Tajik but she looks Pashtun, the tribe of the Taliban, and she speaks their language. So she did a very brave thing.

She took my little brother — because women could not be outside without a man, and even a little boy qualified as a man — and she went to the Taliban's compound. She went right up to them and said, "I want my husband out of jail! Why are you doing this to us? We are poor people. If we had any money, we would have run away!"

By a miracle, they released my father. As soon as he was out, we started walking. We left everything behind in Bamiyan and just walked, for days and days.

We ended up in Kabul. The Taliban were in Kabul, of course, so I don't know why my parents thought it would be safer. Maybe they thought we could hide better in a big city. We went into a little room and stayed there for a long, long time. I forgot all about my school. The world became very small.

But then the Taliban fell and I was able to go back to school. I really wanted my education!

They put me into the fifth grade even though I could barely write my name. I studied really hard and after a year I could read and write properly.

I kept on working hard, and in grade seven I started to learn English. I had some books and I taught myself for a while until my school got a teacher who could help me.

Then, in grade eleven, I got accepted into a program that would pay to let me go to high school in the United States for a year.

I was very excited. I had seen pictures of the United

States, of busy cities with lots of shops and different things to do. But when I got off the plane, I was in Iowa, and all I could see was farmland! That was a bit of a shock.

I stayed with a host family in Iowa. In the beginning I was scared of everyone. My English was not good, and I had heard terrible things about Americans. I had been told that they hated Muslims and liked to shoot each other and did not behave like human beings. But after a couple of weeks I learned that what I'd been told was not the reality.

It took me about three months to get used to the Iowa accent and the people, and then I was fine and comfortable. I even attended church — not because I was forced to but because I wanted to. After all, Jesus is very respected by Muslims. On Saturday nights this church had a youth Bible study, and I went and met some friends there.

The Bible and the Qur'an are very similar. I was glad to learn more about the Bible and I was able to answer the American kids' questions about Islam. So we learned from each other.

For the rest of my time in the US, I was just a normal student. I was happy.

The most special thing about the US is the security. Here in Kabul when I go to the stores I don't feel comfortable, but in the US I could go to the mall all by myself and no one paid any attention to me. No one said, "You should not be out on your own."

The best thing about the United States is that no one cares what you do, so you can do what you want.

After my year in the United States I came back to Afghanistan and enrolled at the American University in Kabul. Now I have been accepted to a program that will pay for me to attend four years of university in the United States. I have applied to Brown in Rhode Island and to a university in Virginia.

When I got accepted to study in the US for a year of high school, my mother was very happy. She never got to go to school, and she loves me to have every opportunity. My father and uncles were not happy. My one uncle said to me, "If you go to the US, you will no longer be my niece. What will people say about me if I allow my niece to go to the US? If you were a boy, maybe. But you are a girl, and I do not allow it."

I remained calm and respectful, but I went to the US without saying goodbye to him. He doesn't talk to me anymore, and we used to be close, so that makes me sad.

My father is happy for me now. At first he was worried about my safety, because of all we had heard about the Americans, but now he is happy. He is not friendly with me the way my mother is, but I know he has a good feeling for me and is proud of me.

I'd like to study international relations and economics, then come back to Afghanistan to serve my country. One day I would like to become an ambassador. And I want to find ways to help other Afghan women.

Women in my country are the ones who suffer a lot. Women like me, who have been given good chances, should help other women and girls.

I am very excited to see what's going to happen next.

Nilab, 15

Until recently, women prisoners were housed in deplorable conditions in Pul-e-Charkhi prison, a beast of a place with a long history of torture and atrocities. Their children were put into the cells with them.

A couple of years ago, the Italian government built a new prison for women — one with better living conditions and that offered a few activities such as handicrafts and literacy. It's better, but it's still a prison — not a good place for the children who live there with their mothers.

In 2009, a home opened up for the children of prisoners. Children live there, go to school, take computer and other courses. They receive counseling to help them deal with the things they have seen in prison and in their lives, and they are taken on outings around the city.

Nilab knows too well what it is like to be in prison. She spent a lot of time there, even though she committed no crime.

I have been in this home for one and a half years. Before that, I lived with my mother in prison.

It was very bad, living in the prison. It is a place where people go to be punished, so it is not a nice place. All the women there have some problems, and these problems mean they don't always get along. Everyone's life is too hard. There are fights, there are arguments, there are people yelling.

I was very small, very young, and it was very bad for me. I was scared every day.

I lived with my mother in one small room, a cell. We were not locked in, but she wanted us to stay in that room, and it wasn't really safe to wander around. There was a mat for her but no mat for me. She was the one in prison. I was just an add-on, so nothing was given to me. My mother got food, but I got no food. My mother shared her portion of food with me, so neither of us had enough to eat. The food was not bad — not good like at this home, but okay. There just wasn't enough of it, and we were hungry all the time. Those mothers with more than one child would have a very bad time.

There was nothing to do all day. No school, no place to play. Just sit in the cell with my mother. She cried every day. She was unhappy about being in prison and worried about me, and about my brother and sister, who were living with my grandmother. Every day, she would cry. It was a burden on me because I could not cheer her up.

She had problems with her health, too. Her teeth hurt and her bones hurt and she could not sleep very well. I got pains in my head.

Before my mother was arrested, I had been to school for a few years. I knew a few things, like reading and some arithmetic. I tried to keep studying in prison, but it was not good. No good light to see by. Lots of noise. And my mother crying all the time.

The guards had a very bad attitude to the prisoners and the children. I don't know why they were so mean. Little children make a lot of noise — that's what they do — and the guards would beat the children for making noise.

My cousin kidnapped a baby. When the police arrested my cousin, my mother was with her, and they arrested her, too. She did not do the kidnapping, but they put her to trial and she got a sentence of six years.

I was with her in the prison for many months and then the commander of the prison came to my mother's cell. He said to her, "Your daughter is too old to be here. If she was a small child, okay, she could stay with you, but she is growing up and should go somewhere else."

That made my mother upset because she had nowhere to send me. My grandparents are poor and it was hard for them to take care of my younger brother and sister. And my father has committed suicide. His family blamed my mother for this, but I don't think that was right. I have very bad memories of my father's suicide. I don't like to talk about it.

The commander of the prison told her about this house, and the head of this house came to the prison to meet us. My mother wasn't sure, but she had no choice, really. The prison said I couldn't stay there any longer.

And so I came here. And I am very happy.

It is a big house, as you can see. It has a high wall around it and guards at the gate so we feel safe. There is a big yard and garden. In the basement there is a big, bright playroom for the smallest kids. I help out down there a lot because the little ones are funny and it is easy to make them happy.

We have dorm rooms where we sleep in bunk beds, a lounge with a TV set — although we don't watch much TV since we have so much studying to do. There is a bit of a library, too. I like to sit there and read when the weather is warm enough. The library is too cold in the winter.

On the first floor, just as you come in, there are classrooms. We have computer classes and English classes and teachers who help us with our homework.

When I first got here I couldn't go to a regular school because I had hardly been to school. I was far behind where I was supposed to be. Plus I was too upset to really study. The teachers here encouraged me, so I started to work really hard and found that I could do it! I can learn and get good grades, and now I am at the top of my class.

But I am not special here for that. None of the kids

had much school when they came here, but the teachers expect everyone to do well and they show us how to work hard. We encourage each other and help each other.

There are kids here that I knew when I was in the prison. They are much happier here.

I've been here long enough now to see how it happens. When kids first come here from the prison all they know how to do is fight. They are afraid and they don't even know how to play. They have to learn everything — how to get clean, how to share, how to eat without trying to grab all the food, how to sleep at night without nightmares, how to play with toys. Some children do not talk at all when they first come here. They are too afraid to talk. It's hard, but they learn, and every day they become happier. The teachers are kind to us. Like mothers.

Now my little brother and sister are here, too. They are also doing very well in school, and I'm happy that we are together.

The food is really good here. All of us like all the food. There is nothing we don't like.

In my future, I plan to be a lawyer and help women who are in trouble with the law. Women are not served well by men. Women have to be able to solve their own problems and not depend on men, because men will not help them.

In prison I met many women who had killed their husbands because they were forced into marriage or their husbands beat them. So they killed their husbands to be free, but they ended up in prison, where they were not free. It's not good enough.

I get to visit my mother every two months. This home does regular visits for all the kids, plus special visits on holidays or if a child is really missing his mother. It's good to visit because otherwise I would worry too much about her. She is not doing well. She stays in her cell a lot, but she says that the guards are treating her better because they can see she is kind.

I like going to the prison with a lot of other children from this home because the mothers are so happy to see us. They look at their children and say, "These are not my children!" because their children have eaten well and are clean and have been to school and so they have lots to talk about.

So, life for me is good right now. It is hard to be away from my mother, and I don't think she should be in prison, but I can't change that. All I can do is watch over my brother and sister and work as hard as I can at my studies. When my mother gets out of prison I want to be able to take care of her and give her a good life.

When that is taken care of, then I will see what else I can do. I have been given a new start. I'm all right. Now I have a responsibility to make others happy.

Sukina, 15

Violence against women in Afghanistan is pervasive because of poverty, the ongoing instability caused by decades of war, and the clinging of many to a system of values that believes women are property and are to be silent and obedient. According to the United Nations, one out of every three Afghan women experiences physical, psychological or sexual violence at the hands of men. Lack of education and economic opportunity for women means that even when laws are in place that respect women's rights, the ability to exercise those rights is limited.

Afghanistan has just a few shelters for women. Supported by international donors, the shelters were operating independently from the government. Early in 2011, the government wanted to bring the shelters — and the women in them — under its control, stating that before an abused woman can enter the shelter she must appear before a panel to state her case. The Afghan Supreme Court also declared that if a woman runs away from her home for reasons of abuse, and she goes to the house of strangers, such as a shelter, she will be arrested and sent to prison on the charge of adultery, because women should go to other family members for help, not to strangers.

But what if a woman's family is also her enemy?

Sukina went into a shelter to save her life.

I came to the shelter to escape my marriage.

I was forced to get married a few years ago.

I grew up in another province. During the Taliban, we became refugees and went to a different province, Wardak, to try to be safe. We lived in a refugee camp there. It was very hard. Then after some years we went back home.

My father is a farmer. He works on other people's land. Because of poverty he had to go into debt with the local shopkeeper to get the things we needed. But then he could not pay the debt. The crops were not good and he did not make enough money. But the shopkeeper had to be paid.

Another man came to my father and said he would pay the shopkeeper. In exchange for doing that, he wanted me to be his wife. I was very young.

I did not know anything about this. No one talked to me about it. I was brought to Kabul to this man's house. I thought he was my uncle. That's how he was introduced to me. He was very old, an old man.

He showed me a white dress and asked me, "Do you like this dress?" I did and I said so. Then he said, "If you like it, put it on. Let's see how you look in it."

So I put it on. Then they put some papers in front of

me and put my thumb on a pad of ink. Then they put my thumbprint on the paper. And with that, I was married.

I was not allowed to go home after that. I belonged to this old man and I had to do what he said. I was so surprised that all this was happening. I thought I was in a bad dream, that my life could not be this.

If he wanted a nice, quiet wife, he did not get one. I was angry and scared and I missed my mother. I cried a lot. Then he would beat me for crying and I cried some more.

My husband's family would not let me see anyone outside the family. They would not let me see my own mother. When neighbors or other visitors came over, they locked me in a back room and threatened to beat me if I made any noise.

They said I had to make carpets to be able to earn some of the money it cost to feed me, and to pay back the money my husband had given to my father for his debt.

There is skill to making carpets. I didn't know how to do it. They would stand over me and wait for me to make a mistake. They would beat me and say, "Why don't you know how to do this?" They locked me in the back room and I was not allowed out into the sunshine.

After a year, my mother came to visit me. When my husband discovered that she was coming, he took a big pair of scissors and cut off my hair. He cut it right off, like I was a boy. He said he did it because it would make me too ashamed to let anybody see me.

When my mother came, I kept my hair covered. I did not let her know what he had done to me. She told me she was not in favor of this marriage but what could she do? She could not go against my father.

My father-in-law ordered me to tell her that I was happy with them and did not want to go home with her. I refused to speak. I could not lie to my mother, but I was too scared to say what was really going on. And because I kept silent, they hit and beat me.

So my mother left without knowing everything that was happening to me.

It went on and on. The beatings, the hunger, the hard times with my husband.

I would cry for days at a time. I cried so much my in-laws would go a little crazy with it. It went on and on.

Finally, one day, when they let me move about more freely so that I could do the chores, I went out into the yard to throw away the garbage. I threw it away and then I kept moving. I ran away. I walked and walked for days and then finally made it home to my mother's house.

She had heard about the Afghan Human Rights Commission. Once I told her about what was going on, and how they were treating me, she found out about how to get in touch with them and she took me to see them. They helped me to get into the women's shelter.

I had to go somewhere safe and hidden. If my husband or his family knew where I was, they might kill me. I am not saying that just to tell my story. They told me they would kill me if I ran away, that I belonged to my husband now and if I left without his permission it would be like I was stealing from him and that was a crime. And if I ran away it would bring shame to my husband's family and to my family.

I didn't want to shame my family, but in the end I wanted to get away and that was all I wanted.

I have been in the shelter now for over two years, waiting for a divorce.

My husband disappeared. He went to some other part of Afghanistan, I think. It is very hard to get a divorce without him. Finally, after waiting for a long time, a lawyer went to my father-in-law. She demanded he produce my husband. When that happens, which I hope will be soon, then I will get my divorce.

The divorce will give me some protection, I hope. It is a legal paper that says I do not belong to my husband anymore. I can show them this paper if they come after me and it will protect me.

I have never been to school. It was not possible when we were refugees, and my family was too poor. It was just not possible. In the shelter, I have been able to attend literacy classes and now I am able to read a bit. And I have helped out in the shelter's kindergarten class. We have a lot of small children staying there. It's good that they get an education while they are young.

In the future I would like to continue to study. The literacy classes have opened a window in my brain, but it is only open a little bit. I want it open all the way because I think I could have a good brain that can do smart things.

When I first came to the shelter I was very weak. My husband's family would punish me by locking me in the back room and not letting me have food. I would not talk to anyone here above a whisper.

And look at me now! I am sitting up straight, looking

you in the eye and telling my story in a loud, clear voice. And you are a stranger. It is my story but it is not the only story. In the shelter I have heard too many stories like mine. We all need to talk about what has happened to us because bad things happen in secret.

I don't know why I left on the day that I did and not on some other day. It was a day like many others. I was throwing away the garbage like I had done before. I had not planned it out. Nothing was packed or prepared. I just threw away the garbage and started walking. I don't think I was brave. I just wasn't ready to die.

Will my father have to pay his debt now? I don't know. It is my father's debt, not mine. I spent years married when I did not want to be. If any of his debt belongs to me, I have paid my portion back.

When the divorce is final and I have the paper, I will go back to my parents' house. I know my mother will be happy to see me and have her with me again.

I don't know how my father will feel.

Shazad, 10

During the 1980s and 1990s, Afghan refugees made up the largest single refugee population on the planet. More than one-fifth of the country fled the war, looking for safety in Pakistan, Iran and any other country that would accept them. Most lived in camps made of mud, tattered tents and rags with few services and little hope.

The United Nations High Commission for Refugees (UNHCR) says that since 2002, more than five million Afghan refugees have returned to their country. In some areas, as many as one out of every three people is a returned refugee. They return to a country still reeling from war and, in many places, still engaged in one.

Returning families need jobs, land, shelter, food and opportunities. Some assistance has been provided by international agencies, but it does not stretch to meet all the needs. In situations like this, children are especially vulnerable. Families in desperate need sell children to traffickers who smuggle them into other countries to act as domestic, sexual or industrial slaves.

There are still 1.7 million Afghan refugees in Pakistan and almost one million still in Iran. Many of the Afghans in Pakistan are in areas badly affected by recent flooding, adding to their misery.

IDP stands for Internally Displaced Person, or internal refugee – a person forced to leave their home area who flees to another part of their country, hoping it will be safer for them there.

The Afghan Ministry of Refugees and Returnees estimates that there are now over 450,000 IDPs in Afghanistan – people who have fled areas where the war is still raging. Many have ended up in makeshift camps on the edge of cities, where they think they will be safe.

These IDP camps have few services like proper latrines or clean water. People freeze in the winter and swelter in the summer heat and dust. People living there try to find work doing anything they can, but it is very difficult. There have been unconfirmed reports of families trying to sell one or more of their

children in order to keep the rest of the family alive.
Shazad and his family are living in an IDP camp
on the edge of Kabul.

We came from Sangin in Helmand Province. A lot of us
in this camp are from that place. Some of the people came
here from Iran. They are Afghans but they lived in Iran
but then Iran told them they had to leave, but they had
no homes to go back to. So they live here.

We left Sangin because of all the fighting. There was
shooting, planes, bombs, lots of soldiers. I didn't like all
the noise. There was a lot of fighting, and no rain, so
nothing would grow and we couldn't eat.

A yard in Shazad's IDP camp.

I think we came here a year ago, maybe a little more. I never went to school in Helmand and I don't go to school here. There is no school in this place.

I'm here with my uncle. He brought me here. I don't know where my parents are. I think they are dead.

I would like to go to school, I think. I don't really know what that would mean, but I think I'd like to do it. It would be something to do.

There's not a lot to do here. There are a lot of children and we play football when we have a ball. When we don't have a ball we use something from the garbage for a ball. Anything that rolls works okay.

The things I don't like about this place? I don't like that it is right by the highway, so there is a lot of noise and smell from the cars and trucks. The air is hard to breathe. We can't play without coughing a lot. Everybody coughs at night, too. It's hard to sleep with all the coughing.

I get cold at night. I sleep in my coat but it is still cold. There are not enough blankets and there is no covering on the floor. Just hard dirt and some paper and things we found in the garbage. It is hard to sleep on. But at least I have shoes. Some kids have no shoes and they can't play very well in winter because their legs and feet hurt.

Sometimes I don't do anything. I sit outside the camp with my back against the mud wall someone built. It's warm there if the sun is shining. I have a friend and we sit there together and look at the cars going by and decide which ones we like. I want to have a car some day. Maybe a red one.

We get water from a pump. We have to carry it a long

way. That's one of my jobs. It's heavy to carry but it's something to do.

There are animals here and they smell, but at least it is a farm smell. It's a smell like from my home.

I want to go home if the war stops. It is nice there. They grow a lot of poppies and they are beautiful. I want to be back in my home. I want to breathe normal again.

The things I like about this place are there is no war or shooting. We see helicopters but they don't shoot at us, they just fly around. And most of the adults here are nice if we don't make too much noise and they are not too worried. If someone gets some food they usually share it.

A baby was born here yesterday. I've seen her. She's very tiny. When she cries it is not very loud. She'll get louder.

We look through garbage piles to find things to burn to stay warm. Sometimes we find food like old bread, or something we can use, but not often. People usually throw away what they don't want. Some of the food is bad and we feed it to the sheep. They eat anything.

Some people have taken up the work of making bird-cages and raising birds. It doesn't take long to grow a bird, so that's a good job. They make the cages from sticks tied together. People buy the birds for good luck or maybe to eat. I don't know. I might do that job some day.

That's if I can't go back to Helmand. How long does war last? I don't want to still be here when I'm old.

Sara, 17

Economic power is vital for women everywhere to be able to control their destiny. Assisting women to start up small businesses, like handicrafts, bee-keeping, poultry-raising and tailoring is a way that women can earn money and improve the lives of themselves and their children.

Sara benefits from having both a grandmother and a mother who are astute businesswomen.

My grandmother is a businesswoman. My mother is a businesswoman. And I am going to be a businesswoman.

My grandmother runs a project for widows to make jewelry out of the stones of Afghanistan, like lapis lazuli, a famous blue stone.

My mother works with 350 farm women from all around Afghanistan. They produce grapes and raisins from the grapes, walnuts, almonds, things like that. My mother finds markets for what they produce so that they can earn money.

We stayed in Afghanistan during part of the Taliban times. We stayed inside all the time, trying to study and pass the time. One day my grandmother got sick. There was only one burqa in the house. My mother gave it to my grandmother to wear and my mother wore a chador over her head. That wasn't good enough for the Taliban and they beat her very badly. After that, we decided to get out and all go to Pakistan.

Things were hard there. My mother worked as a cleaner in the home of a Pakistani couple. But my mother is always looking out for something better, and she got money from an aid organization to start a small school for refugee children who had to work making carpets during the day.

My mother went back to Afghanistan a few years after the Taliban fell. She left us in Pakistan because she wanted to see for herself that we would be all right and could go to school. She likes to take charge and make things happen. She got a job with the Afghan Women's Business Council, rented an apartment, and we came back to Afghanistan.

I was afraid because I had bad memories of Afghanistan under the Taliban. One night we were in our home and we were talking, entertaining ourselves because there was nothing else to do. Someone said something funny and we all laughed. But then the Taliban started banging on the window.

We knew it was the Taliban, even though the window was painted over, because they yelled at us and told us to stop laughing, that our laughter was bothering the men who were walking along the road. We could not even laugh in our own home!

But it didn't matter that I was afraid to come back. We came back and started our lives again in Kabul.

Kabul is okay. It's my home, but I don't really like living here. I'd prefer to live in Germany.

My uncle is in Germany. My mother's brother. I don't know which city. I've never been there but I have learned a lot about it. It seems like a clean place where things work and the trees are green. Here the trees are covered in dust all the time. Kabul is very dusty from all the cars and all the building that is going on. Plus, here there are a lot of soldiers and guns in the streets. Even if something bad isn't happening, you can easily think that something bad is about to happen. And bombs go off and people blow themselves up and everyone panics. Things like that don't happen in Germany.

I don't know what started my mother on this newest business. She sees things that aren't being done and finds a way to do them. She travels all over Afghanistan to meet with farm women and collect the things they grow. She wants to start making almond butter to sell in foreign countries because Afghanistan grows good almonds.

I am now in grade twelve, plus I take extra courses to

improve my English. Even though I want to live in Germany where they speak German, knowing English will be good for my future. I am also going to take prep classes for university entrance exams so I can get a good score.

I have no time for fun! It's always work — school work or helping to take care of my younger brothers and sisters.

When I do have a bit of time, my friends and I like to play sports. We can't usually run around much — there is no space for that — so we jump rope a lot, which is good exercise and we can do it in a small space.

My mother goes to many insecure parts of Afghanistan to meet with her farm women, and I worry about her a lot. Sometimes I go with her. I see how hard their lives are, even with my mother's help. The government of Afghanistan has declared Thursday and Friday to be the weekend, when people can take a break from work and have a holiday. But there are no holidays for women!

I plan to go into business and my friends have the same plan. We want to make a lot of money. It's good for Afghan women to make a lot of money. With money we have power. We are going into business so that we can control our own lives.

Shaharazad, 12

Fawzia Koofi is a formidable woman — smart, energetic, strong and determined that Afghanistan's future will be better than its past. She is raising her daughter, Shaharazad, to be the next generation of strong Afghan women.

I met Shaharazad in the lobby of the Intercontinental Hotel in Kabul. This famous hotel, on the top of a hill, has a small army of security police checking and re-checking everyone who approaches and enters the hotel. In spite of the precautions, in the spring of 2011, the hotel was attacked by Taliban gunmen. Several people were killed.

I am named after a famous storyteller. My mother is Fawzia Koofi, a member of the Afghan parliament. She was elected by the people of Badakhshan, the province near China. They had a choice of people to vote for and they thought she would do the best job so they voted for her.

Her father — my grandfather — was also a member of parliament a long time ago, in the 1970s. I never met him. He was murdered when my mother was still small. He owned the only radio in the whole area, although that's not why he was killed. Before he died he had seven wives and twenty-three children.

My mother was the first girl in her family to go to school. She was in university when the Taliban came. She had to quit. All the girls had to quit.

She always tells my sister and me, "You are so lucky to be young women now instead of being young women in those days! We could not go out, we could not study, we could not have fun." I'm glad I didn't live through that, but that doesn't mean my life now is easy.

My father died when I was small, just like my mother's father did. He was arrested by the Taliban and got tuberculosis in prison and that's how he died. He was an engineer and a science teacher.

Having my mother be a member of parliament is very nice, but it also scares me. I get afraid for her safety. Maybe something will happen to her and then we won't have her.

I was with her one day when she was attacked. This was last year.

It was on the road between Kabul and Jalalabad. Because she's a member of parliament she always travels with bodyguards. They follow along in another car and sit with her in our car. I was in the back seat of our car eating a bag of chips. I used to like eating them but since the attack I don't like them anymore. I was eating these chips when the cars were stopped and all this shooting started. Men were shooting at us! The bodyguards were shooting at them and were trying to protect my mother and us. I was so scared! I didn't know what was happening and I didn't want to get shot. There was so much confusion.

Then a helicopter came and we got put into the helicopter and taken to a clinic, but we were all okay, just scared. But two policemen died that day.

That's the only bad part about my mother being a member of parliament. All the danger. Sometimes she travels in helicopters and the helicopters are really old, so that's another thing I worry about.

The best part about her being a member of parliament is we get to come here, to the Intercontinental Hotel. It's a very fancy hotel high up on a hill. There is lots of security to get through to get in — lots of guards on the hill on the way up and guards to check your bags as you go inside. So it's safe. That's a good thing.

All the members of parliament have rooms here because they need a place to stay when they're working. Some of the MPs have children who come with them and so we play together all over the hotel. My mother knows we are safe here, so while she's busy in meetings, my sister and I and our friends go all over the hotel. The staff know us and like us because we have fun but we don't cause trouble. We sit in the lounges and ride the elevators and go exploring. We go to each other's rooms and play games on our computers. Some of the MPs come from provinces where there are no good schools and their children don't know about computers and things. We teach them what we know. And we watch television and run through the gardens.

I don't like shouting and loud noises and I don't like seeing men with guns in the street. That's hard because everywhere you look in Kabul there are men with guns. They're supposed to be there to protect us but I never know if they'll start shooting at us instead.

My mother says my generation is the hope for Afghanistan. My sister and I wear jeans and go to school and we hear her stories about how hard it was but we don't really understand it. My mother says we should know about the past but think more about the future.

My message to other kids? Tell them I want to live with them in a peaceful world and a peaceful country and be happy with my mother and family.

Miriam, 14

UNICEF estimates that there are 1.6 million orphans now in Afghanistan. War, disease and poverty have taken the lives of many parents. Some of these children are taken in by family members who care deeply about them. Others are not so lucky. They end up on the street or in situations of danger and exploitation.

Miriam lives in a girls' orphanage that is supported by Canadian donors. There is uncertainty about her future. It is next to impossible for women to live alone in Afghanistan, and without families to arrange a marriage, it is difficult to find a partner in life. Education is the best hope that Miriam and the girls she lives with will have for a safe and happy life once they become too old to stay at the orphanage.

I have been in this orphanage for six years. We were in another building up until two years ago, but the landlord sold the house and we had to move to this house. Before I came to Afghanistan I lived in an orphanage in Pakistan.

My mother is still alive. She is very poor. She has no job and her life is very bad. She cannot afford to have her children with her. My sister and I are in this orphanage. My brother is in another place. I get to see my mother once a month. She is staying in the home of my uncle. There is no room for us there.

There are thirty girls in this orphanage. Some have lost both parents, some have lost one parent. The youngest is a little baby who has no parents. Then there are some little girls in kindergarten, some older, and some even older. I'm not the oldest, but I'm close to being the oldest.

People in Canada send us presents, like books and toys and stuffed animals. We live in a big house. There are bedrooms upstairs with several bunk beds in each room. We each have a metal box where we can keep our things. There is a room with big tables where we eat and do our homework, and a room we call the winter room because it is the only room that's warm in the winter. It has a rug on the floor, toshaks along the walls and a woodstove. That's where we spend most of our time. The little ones roll around on the floor, the older ones like me read and talk and play games and try different ways to do our hair.

The winter room has a television set but our house-mother doesn't let us watch it very much. She says our time is better spent studying. When we get to watch, I like Bollywood movies. We also have a shelf full of books, both for little kids and for older girls. Most of the books are in English. We are all learning English. I'm reading an English book now by Judy Blume. I have to go slow because my English is still not good.

We used to play a game where we would sit in front of the window of one of the bedrooms that looks out over the street. We would sit there and wave at people who walked past and see if they waved back. It was a game to see if we could make them wave. But some men came to the gate and told our housemother that we had to stop that game or he would have the police come. So we can't play that game anymore.

But we have other things we can do. We have been to the zoo, we can jump rope in the backyard. We can work on our memory books. We all have a notebook we use to keep our memories in. Some use them for writing, some use them for drawing. I like to keep pictures of my favor-ite movie stars in mine, so I don't forget them.

When girls come into this orphanage they usually just stay. It's very hard for Afghan girls to manage in the world unless they are married. I am taking extra classes at school because I'd like to go to university. That would give me a good future.

There was a girl who lived here but she left to get mar-ried. Her uncle showed up and said he had a husband for

The backyard of Miriam's orphanage.

her. She didn't want to get married. She wanted to finish school. We didn't want her to go, but our housemother couldn't stop him from taking her away. So she had to leave and marry someone she didn't know in another province. I wonder if she is okay.

I think I would like to be a doctor. That would be a good job. Or I might be a teacher. Or I could be a singer.

Maybe I'll be all three.

Anonymous girl, 14

The United Nations reports that between 60 and 80 percent of all marriages in Afghanistan are forced. The marriage is imposed upon the girl whether she wants to be married or not. Marriage of daughters is used to repay debts, solve a dispute or pay family expenses. The father of the bride is given money by the groom's family in exchange for the marriage.

Although there are laws on the books against forced marriage — and against child marriage — the laws are seldom enforced. In rural Afghanistan, girls are mostly married off between the ages of seven and eleven and, according to Tahera Nassrat of the Foreign Policy Association, rarely does a girl reach her sixteenth birthday without being married.

Forced child marriage usually leads to a miserable life for these girls — a life involving rape, childbirth before their bodies and minds are ready for it, health problems, abuse, isolation, depression, lack of educational opportunities and endless hard labor.

The girls' prison in Kabul is full of young teens who are paying the price for trying to take ownership over their own lives.

Both of my parents are alive. My father is a police officer with the ministry of the interior. My mother stays at home. I have five brothers and three sisters.

I've been in the prison for six months.

My father arranged a marriage for me with a cousin of his, a very old man.

I did not want to marry this old man. I am young, so of course I want to marry someone who is also young. I told my father this. I told my father and my mother and neighbors and anyone who might listen. But my father was determined that this was who I should marry.

What I really wanted to do was to continue my studies. I wanted to study law, because being a lawyer would be a good job for a woman in Afghanistan.

My future now? Probably nothing. No future.

So I did not want to marry this old man. There are supposed to be laws that protect girls from forced marriages. I learned about these laws in school. A woman in our district worked for the ministry of women's affairs. I went to her and asked for help. She said she could not help me.

I had to find my own help.

There was a boy who worked at the local radio station. He was on the radio and he played songs and took phone calls from people who wanted to hear a particular song. I used to call in to the radio station to ask for my favorite songs. He liked the sound of my voice, I guess, and he got my phone number from when I called in and he called me back. We started talking that way, and when I told him about the marriage I was being forced into, he said he could help me.

We met up and he took me away into another province. I thought everything was going to be fine. I would miss my family but I thought that in time they would forgive me and I could see them again. I thought I could just go to another place and start school there and live my life and everything would be okay.

We were getting something to eat in a restaurant. The manager of this restaurant started asking us questions about who we were and where we came from and where we were going. We thought he was just having a conversation, but he ended up calling the police. They came to the restaurant and arrested us there.

The police separated us. We went to a district police station and eventually I was brought here.

I had to go on trial. I was charged with running away. It was very scary. All these men were in the courtroom, looking at me and talking about me. I was not allowed to speak. There was a defense attorney who spoke for me. He was very good and kind to me, but I wish I could have said something. After all, it's my life.

In primary court I was given the sentence of seven and a half years. The boy got five years. In secondary court my sentence was upheld, and the boy got his reduced to three years.

He got less time because my father came to court and testified that this was all my fault so the court should punish me more.

After the trial there was a jerga, a meeting of men in the community to decide what should happen because the old man had been promised a bride. He felt he was owed a bride and the jerga agreed. They said he should get my ten-year-old sister since he couldn't have me.

I was very afraid for my sister but then something good happened. The old man committed suicide. So my little sister did not have to marry him.

My father blames me for his cousin's suicide, but I don't care. I'm not responsible for what some old man does.

I don't see my father anymore. He never comes to see me. My mother comes once a week. She did not want me to be married off. She wanted me to continue in school. But she has no voice in the family.

Here it is not so bad. It is a prison, but they have a teacher who comes in so we can go to school for a little bit each day. And no one is making me get married when I don't want to.

We have a routine here that is easy to follow. We have school in the morning until eleven. Did you hear us singing when you came in? Between eleven and one we have lunch and prayers. Then in the afternoon we sometimes have courses. People come in from the outside and teach us beauty parlor or tailoring. I'd like to learn English and computers — and law, of course — but whatever I get in here is more than I would be getting if I hadn't run away.

On Thursdays and Fridays we have days off from school. We can take care of personal things like laundry or mending. Some girls do handicrafts like ribbon work. I'd like it if we could do art classes because I like to draw.

We get outside for one hour a day, but inside we are not confined. We can go upstairs, go into each other's rooms. All the rooms have bunk beds, like this one, with lots of girls sharing. They are not crowded, and there are big windows so the rooms are bright. I'm friends with some of the girls. Most of them are also in here for running away. I don't know of anyone who is in here for thieving or hurting anyone.

When I turn twenty I will be sent to the adult women's prison. I don't like to think about that. It's still a far time away. After that, I don't know. My father won't want me back. I don't know where I'll go.

Sigrullah, 14

Libraries save lives.

They saved my life as a teenager growing up in Paris, Ontario, giving me a glimpse of something big and glorious to reach for.

They save the lives of people around the world by giving us examples of how great we humans can be. They fill our heads with new ideas and information, and they reassure us that, whatever mud we are wading through in our present lives, there is the possibility of something better.

Chilsitoon is an impoverished neighborhood in Kabul. The Afghan Women's Resource Centre has built a community center there, with a small gym where women can exercise in safety, classrooms for handicrafts, literacy, human-rights education and small-business training.

And a library.

Sigrullah is on the Chilsitoon children's committee.

My father is a carpenter. He works in a furniture shop, making frames for beds, tables, things like that, when he is well. Right now he is sick so he is not working. I work as a tailor's helper. It brings in some money and so our family eats. I am learning to be a proper tailor so that I can earn even more money. But that is not really the kind of work I want to do.

I really want to be an electrical engineer because there are not a lot of people in Afghanistan who can do that kind of work. It would be easy to find a good job. I would like to bring electricity to all of Afghanistan because when people have electric lights, it is good for their eyes to study at night. Most people work all day and the only time they can sit with a book is at night. So they need electric lights.

I might also be a doctor because Afghanistan needs doctors. A lot of kids here want to be teachers because to be a teacher is holy work.

I am a member of the Chilsitoon children's committee. The people who run this center told everyone they were looking for children to do this job. I thought it would be a good thing to do, so I applied and I was chosen. It's a volunteer job. We don't get paid.

This is a very poor area of Kabul so people have a lot of problems. People come here from all parts of Afghanistan because Kabul is the capital city. They think it will be very nice, very safe, with good jobs. I am from Parwan province. Another committee member is from Paktia. We come from all over.

In this committee we learn about children's rights and human rights. We learn about what the law says people should and should not do. We talk about what rights parents have and what people should do for their country.

Children in this area have a lot of problems. It is our job to find out what the problems are and to see if we can fix them. We talk to the children who come here for courses and ask them, "How is your life? Are you happy? Are you being well treated?" We also ask children these questions when we meet them in the neighborhood outside the center.

They have a lot of problems because they are poor. Their parents get upset and hit them, or there is no food in the house, or they want to come to courses in the center and their parents won't allow it. We will hear about a girl who is being forced to marry someone she doesn't want to. These are big problems, bigger than we can solve.

But we can talk to children about their rights and the law and sometimes we can explain things to their parents. We discuss things with the adults who run the center and they can sometimes talk to the parents and help them out with food or find out what's making them angry.

It doesn't always work, but sometimes it does. They go to the local mullahs and say, "Too many parents are hitting their children in this neighborhood. Can you preach about that in the mosque?" And the mullahs will talk about how Islam is a religion of peace and that children should be protected.

We try to keep the neighborhood clean. We go door to door and tell people not to throw their garbage into the streets because that brings rats and flies and those things are not good for children.

I would like all the streets in Kabul to be cleaner. Many of us have to walk a long way to come to this center every day. The streets are very dusty and lots of children become sick from the dust. I would like to know how we can fix this problem.

There are a lot of people who come to this center, all ages. Ladies come here who are widows, and they learn how to read and make pickles to sell. There is a room upstairs that they use for exercise and games. It's easy for boys to play games and run around — we can do that anywhere. It's harder for ladies.

I like that we can work together to solve our problems. Talking helps a lot. We had a public meeting here about the space between parents and children. Children don't tell their parents about their problems and parents don't talk to their children. It makes problems worse when we don't talk.

My favorite part of this center is this library. We have ten shelves of books! Wonderful books, all different books. We need to have different books because we all have different minds. I like books about Afghan history. Some people like books about cooking or poetry or law.

I am happiest when I am in this library. All of our problems can be solved with these books.

Afghanistan will have a good future if the government will help all the people learn to read and if every community could have a good library so they could find solutions and solve their own problems.

About Afghanistan

Afghanistan is a small country that lies between Europe and Asia. It contains mountain ranges, fast-flowing rivers and golden deserts. Its fertile valleys once produced an abundance of fruit, wheat and vegetables.

Throughout history, explorers and traders have passed through Afghanistan and tried to control it for their own interests. The country has been more or less continuously at war since 1978, when American-backed fighters opposed the Soviet-supported government. In 1980, the Soviet Union invaded Afghanistan, and the war escalated, with the United States backing Afghan freedom fighters, many of whom were warlords. The fighting was fierce, cruel and prolonged.

After the Soviets were defeated in 1989, a civil war erupted, as various groups fought for control of the country. Millions of Afghans became refugees, and many still live in huge camps in Pakistan, Iran and Russia. Many people have spent their whole lives in these camps, and millions of Afghans have been killed, maimed or blinded.

The Taliban militia, one of the groups that the US and Pakistan once funded, trained and armed, took control of the capital city of Kabul in September 1996. They imposed extremely restrictive laws on girls and women.

Children looking through rubbish for something they can use.

Schools for girls were closed down, women were no longer allowed to hold jobs, and strict dress codes were enforced. Books were burned, televisions smashed, and music in any form was forbidden.

In the fall of 2001, al-Qaeda, a terrorist group based in Afghanistan and protected by the Taliban, launched attacks on the Pentagon and the World Trade Center in New York City. In response, the United States led a coalition of nations into bombing Afghanistan and drove the Taliban from power. Elections were held and a new government and constitution were set up. A number of schools for boys and girls were opened, and about half of Afghan children now have access to some form of schooling. In some parts of the country, women were allowed back into the work force.

Women and children in a Kabul marketplace.

However, Afghanistan is far from being a nation of peace, for many reasons. The Taliban has returned to fight a very effective guerrilla war against the government and foreign forces. Afghanistan has become a major producer of opium, from which heroin is made. There is a great deal of corruption at all levels of government. Finally, Afghans, like people around the world, are uncomfortable with foreign forces fighting in their country. Struggles for women's rights continue as well, with girls' schools being burned and women activists being assassinated.

There are no easy answers for the people of Afghanistan as they face such a difficult situation. Learning more about this beautiful, tragic country and its wonderful people is one small way to try to avoid the many mistakes outsiders have made that have brought Afghans to this difficult time in their history.

For Further Information

Organizations

Afghan Book House
An organization founded by two librarians to promote librarianship, reading and the local publishing of Afghan books.

Afghanistan Youth Center www.ayc.8m.net
An Afghan youth organization in Kabul.

Afghan Youth Initiative www.afghanyouth.org
An organization that supports Afghan youth in Kabul.

Aina www.ainaworld.org
Former publishers of *Parvaz*, the only children's magazine in Afghanistan, Aina now works in partnership with Aschiana to provide writing, photojournalism and reading training to Afghan children.

Aschiana Foundation www.aschiana-foundation.org
An organization that provides food, education, drug counseling, job training and micro-credit to street children.

Canadian Women for Women in Afghanistan
www.cw4wafghan.ca
Supports educational opportunities for Afghan women and their families.

International Board on Books for Young People (IBBY)
www.ibby.org
IBBY is working with Afghans to create an Afghan National IBBY

section that would house a major center for reading promotion and train Afghans in reading promotion, writing, illustrating and publishing of local children's books.

Little Women for Little Women in Afghanistan
www.littlewomenforlittlewomen.com
Founded by Alaina Podmorow, this kid-run organization raises money for Afghan schools and orphanages. Members produced a book (*Through Our Eyes*) of their own poetry next to images of girls from an Afghan orphanage. They welcome new members and branches.

Noor Educational and Capacity Development Organization
www.necdo.org.af
Provides women, youth and children in Kabul, Ghazni and Jalalabad with health, literacy, vocational, internet, English-language and other educational support.

PARSA www.afghanistan-parsa.org
Since 1996, PARSA has been working in Afghanistan with war victims, widows, orphans and other disadvantaged people.

Revolutionary Association of the Women of Afghanistan
www.rawa.org
Started in 1977, RAWA advocates political action, runs schools and supports women's rights.

Shuhada www.shuhada.org.af
Begun in 1989 by Dr. Sima Samar, Shuhada works to improve health, education and women's rights in Afghanistan and in the refugee camps.

SOLA School of Leadership Afghanistan
www.sola-afghanistan.org
An NGO that provides educational opportunities to train Afghanistan's future leaders.

Women for Afghan Women www.womenforafghanwomen.org
A human rights organization based in New York and Kabul. Recently opened two new Children's Support Centers where children whose mothers are in prison can live and attend school.

Books

(although written for adults, the following books are suitable for grade 8 and up):

A Bed of Red Flowers: In Search of My Afghanistan by Nelofer Pazira, Random House, 2005. A filmmaker recounts her life through the many stages of war in Afghanistan.

Kabul in Winter: Life Without Peace in Afghanistan by Ann Jones, Metropolitan/Henry Holt, 2006. An American aid worker tells the stories of women in Afghanistan since the fall of the Taliban, and describes how little has changed.

My Forbidden Face – Growing Up Under the Taliban: A Young Woman's Story by Latifa, Virago, 2002. Writing under a fake name, sixteen-year-old Latifa tells the story of how she survived in Taliban-controlled Afghanistan.

Veiled Threat: The Hidden Power of the Women of Afghanistan by Sally Armstrong, Penguin, 2002. A Canadian journalist writes about her trips to Afghanistan and the women who have affected her with their stories of survival and resistance.

Women of the Afghan War by Deborah Ellis, Praeger, 2000. Interviews with Afghan women living in refugee camps in Pakistan and Russia.

Glossary

afghani – The currency of Afghanistan. One Canadian dollar is the rough equivalent of 45 afghanis.

Allah – The Islamic name for God.

al-Qaeda – A network of terrorists who believe in a radical, and un-Islamic, version of Islam.

Buddha – Siddhartha Gautama, the founder of the Buddhist religion, who lived around 400 BC.

burqa – A long tent-like garment worn by women. It covers the entire body and has a narrow mesh screen over the eyes.

chador – A piece of cloth worn by women and girls to cover their hair and shoulders.

Communist – Someone who believes in the philosophy of Communism — that people should contribute according to their individual abilities and receive according to their needs.

Dari – One of the two main languages spoken in Afghanistan.

despot – Someone who holds onto absolute power, often in a brutal way.

djinn – An invisible spirit, a supernatural being.

exiles – Individuals who are banned from living in their native country.

guerrilla – An armed fighter in a small military group.

hafiz (pl. huffaz) – A Muslim who can recite the entire Qur'an from memory.

hashish – A black tar-like substance made from the marijuana plant.

heroin – An illegal, addictive narcotic made from a certain kind of poppy.

insurgents – A group that uses military force to oppose a government.

Islam – A religion that follows the holy book of the Qur'an and the teachings of the Prophet Muhammad.

land mine – A bomb planted in the ground, so it explodes if it is stepped on.

Maristoon – An Afghan term that refers to a place where destitute people can find help and refuge.

mosque – A place where Muslims go to pray.

mullah – A religious expert and teacher of Islam.

Muslim – Someone who follows the religion of Islam.

nan – Afghan flatbread.

NATO – North Atlantic Treaty Organization, an alliance of North American and European countries formed after World War II.

NGO – Non-governmental organization.

opium – An illegal drug made from a kind of poppy.

Pashtu – One of the two main languages spoken in Afghanistan.

Qur'an – The holy book of Islam, believed to be the word of God as revealed to the Prophet Muhammad.

refugees – People who must leave their home country because their lives are in danger.

Soviet – A citizen of the former Soviet Union or USSR (Union of Soviet Socialist Republics), including Russia and other Communist countries.

surah – A chapter or section of the Qur'an.

Taliban – The army that took over Afghanistan in September 1996. Although it was forced from power at the end of 2011, it continues to fight against the government and foreign forces.

terrorist – Someone who uses violence or the threat of violence to force others to behave in a certain way. In general, terrorists target civilian populations.

toshak – A narrow mattress used in Afghan homes as a chair or bed.

tuberculosis – A contagious bacterial infection that usually attacks the lungs.

UN – The United Nations, an international organization that promotes peace, security and economic development.

UNHCR – The United Nations High Commission on Refugees.

UNICEF – The United Nations International Children's Emergency Fund, an agency that helps governments (especially in developing countries) improve the health and education of children and mothers.

visa – A document that allows a person to enter another country.

warlord – A military commander who acts in his own interests rather than in the interests of the national government.

About the Author

Deborah Ellis is best known for her Breadwinner Trilogy, set in Afghanistan and Pakistan — a series that has been published in twenty-five languages, with more than one million dollars in royalties donated to Canadian Women for Women in Afghanistan and Street Kids International. She has won the Governor General's Award, the Ruth Schwartz Award, the University of California's Middle East Book Award, Sweden's Peter Pan Prize, the Jane Addams Children's Book Award and the Vicky Metcalf Award for a Body of Work. She recently received the Ontario Library Association's President's Award for Exceptional Achievement, and she has been named to the Order of Ontario.

Deborah lives in Simcoe, Ontario.